KANT AND SKEPTICISM

PRINCETON MONOGRAPHS
IN PHILOSOPHY

—— · ꟼMP · ——

The Princeton Monographs in Philosophy series offers short
historical and systematic studies on a wide variety
of philosophical topics.

KANT AND
SKEPTICISM

Michael N. Forster

PRINCETON UNIVERSITY PRESS

PRINCETON AND OXFORD

Copyright © 2008 by Princeton University Press
Published by Princeton University Press, 41 William Street,
Princeton, New Jersey 08540
In the United Kingdom: Princeton University Press,
3 Market Place, Woodstock, Oxfordshire OX20 1SY

Library of Congress Cataloging-in-Publication Data

Forster, Michael N.
Kant and skepticism / Michael N. Forster.
Includes bibliographical references and index.
ISBN 978-0-691-12987-7 (hardcover : alk. paper)
1. Kant, Immanuel, 1724–1804. 2. Skepticism. I. Title.
B2799.S5467 2008
149'.7309—dc22   2007020800

British Library Cataloging-in-Publication Data is available

This book has been composed in Janson Text

Printed on acid-free paper. ∞

press.princeton.edu

Printed in the United States of America

1 3 5 7 9 10 8 6 4 2

For Noha

WITH MUCH LOVE

Contents

Preface

THIS ESSAY concerns Kant and skepticism. It is a sort of companion piece to earlier work of mine on Hegel and skepticism: *Hegel and Skepticism* (1989) and *Hegel's Idea of a Phenomenology of Spirit* (1998), chapter 3. In many ways the two projects ascribe very different positions to Kant and Hegel. However, they do identify one large and important piece of common ground which the two philosophers share: a profound preoccupation with *Pyrrhonian* skepticism. The identification of this form of skepticism as a central concern for Hegel was probably the most striking feature of the earlier project. Likewise, the identification of it as a central concern for Kant—and as the source of a full-blooded *crise pyrrhonienne* which Kant underwent in *Dreams of a Spirit Seer, Illustrated by Dreams of Metaphysics* (1766)—will probably be found the most striking feature of the present essay. My purpose in this essay is to consider Kant's position on its own terms, rather than to compare it with Hegel's. However, the final chapter does stage a confrontation of sorts between their positions.

Versions of this essay have been in existence for about twenty years now, and I have incurred many debts of gratitude in the course of its development. I would especially like to thank the following people, who went to the trouble of providing detailed, probing written comments which helped me to improve the material significantly: Michael Inwood, Béatrice Longuenesse, and Allen Wood. I would also like to thank the following people for contributing to its development in various ways: Fred Beiser, Eckhart Förster, Michael Frede, Gottfried Gabriel, Don Garrett, Steven Stich, and the late Manley Thompson. In addition, I would like to thank audiences at the following institutions who listened and responded to parts of it given as public presentations: the University of Chicago, Princeton University, the Friedrich Schiller University in Jena, and New York University. I would also like to thank the many generations of students at the University of Chicago who have listened and responded to versions of it presented as lectures over the years. I would like to thank Ian Malcolm and his colleagues at the Princeton University Press for their excellent work and friendliness. Last but not least, I would like to thank my parents Michael and Kathleen, my wife Noha, and my daughter Alya for their unfailing love, support, and patience.

Kant's works are cited in this essay in the following conventional ways: in the case of the *Critique of Pure Reason*, by means of the standard system of A and B numbers for the first and second editions respectively (e.g., A90 / B123); in the case of other texts, normally by means of the volume and page number of the standard German edition of Kant's works published by the Königliche Preussische Akademie der Wissenschaften, generally known as the *Akademieausgabe* and hence referred to here as AA (e.g., AA 4:247), or when a text is frequently cited, after a first citation, simply by means of the page number of the relevant volume of that edition. Thanks largely to the excellent new Cambridge Edition of Kant's works edited by Paul Guyer and Allen Wood, these forms of reference should allow readers working with English translations to locate passages easily, while also permitting readers working with German texts to do so. Translations are either my own or borrowed from standard English editions of Kant's works, sometimes with modifications (mainly editions by Norman Kemp Smith and Lewis White Beck).

KANT AND SKEPTICISM

•ꟼMꟹ•

I

Exposition

CHAPTER ONE

Varieties of Skepticism

IN THE FIRST part of this essay I shall give a general exposition of the role of skepticism in Kant's critical philosophy. In the second part, I shall offer a critical assessment of the Kantian position that emerges.

The critical philosophy, as first set forth by Kant in the *Critique of Pure Reason* of 1781/7 (henceforth: the *Critique*), grew from and addresses a very complex set of philosophical concerns. But among these, two which stand out as especially central are a concern to address *skepticism* and a concern to develop a reformed *metaphysics*.

That much is widely recognized. However, it is a fundamental thesis of the present essay that these two projects belong tightly together, namely in the following sense: The types of skepticism which really originated and motivate the critical philosophy are types of skepticism that mainly *threaten metaphysics*;[1] and conversely, what originated and motivates the critical philosophy's reform of metaphysics is above all an aspiration to enable metaphysics to *withstand skepticism*.[2]

To amplify a little on the first of those points: Treatments of Kant have commonly been plagued, it seems to me, by two closely connected weaknesses—a failure to distinguish with sufficient care between different types of skepticism, and a (largely consequent) failure to discern the different roles that different types of skepticism played in connection with the origination and motivation of the critical philosophy. For the purposes of

interpreting Kant, it is especially important to distinguish between the following three sorts of skepticism: First, there is
"veil of perception" skepticism, or skepticism concerning the legitimacy of inferring from the existence and character of one's
mental representations to the existence and character of a
mind-external world (this tends to be the very paradigm of
skepticism for most Anglophone philosophers). "Veil of perception" skepticism is not especially targeted at the claims of
metaphysics (though they are *among* its targets). Second, there
is *Humean skepticism*, or skepticism concerning (1) the existence
of concepts not derivable from corresponding sensible impressions (in Kant's idiom: a priori concepts), and (2) knowledge of
propositions neither true simply in virtue of logical law nor
known from experience (in Kant's idiom: synthetic a priori
knowledge). Both of these forms of Humean skepticism are ex-
emplified in Hume's treatment of causation. This Humean type
of skepticism does have a special bearing on metaphysics due
to the prevalence of such putative concepts and such putative
knowledge within metaphysics. Third, there is *Pyrrhonian skepticism*, a skepticism which, in the manner of the ancient Pyrrhonists, motivates suspension of judgment by establishing a balance of opposing arguments, or "equipollence" (*isostheneia*). As
Kant interprets it, this ancient form of skepticism too has a
special bearing on metaphysics.

It turns out, I shall argue, that of these three types of skepticism, the first, "veil of perception" skepticism, played no significant role at all in the origination of the critical philosophy
and only a secondary role in its mature motivation (despite the
fact that it is already present in the first edition of the *Critique*
and rises to some prominence in the second edition). The second type, Humean skepticism, did play an important role in
originating the critical philosophy, in virtue of its special bearing on the tenability of metaphysics, namely some time in or
shortly after 1772, and also remained central to the critical philosophy's mature motivation (facts reflected in Kant's famous
remarks about it near the start of the *Prolegomena to Any Future
Metaphysics* of 1783 [henceforth: *Prolegomena*]). But it was actually the third type, Pyrrhonian skepticism, which, again in vir-

tue of a perceived special bearing on metaphysics, first really shook Kant's faith in the precritical discipline of metaphysics, namely in the mid-1760s, and thence eventually led to the reform of metaphysics undertaken by the critical philosophy, and which (like Humean skepticism) also remained at the heart of the mature motivation of the critical philosophy.

In its first and third parts, this interpretation will strike many scholars of Kant, especially in the Anglophone tradition, as heresy (or worse).[3] This is one reason why it has seemed to me to be worth articulating.

To amplify a little on the second point made above (that what originated and motivates the critical philosophy's reform of metaphysics is above all an aspiration to enable it to withstand skepticism): I shall argue that the key features which define the distinctive character of the reformed metaphysics at which Kant ultimately arrives in the critical philosophy—including, not only its specific conceptual and propositional contents, but also its status as a priori rather than supersensuous, its status as transcendentally ideal, and its systematicity—are all built into it mainly in order to enable it to withstand skepticism. And I shall argue that Kant has in the critical philosophy an elaborate set of strategies dependent on these features for actually defending his reformed metaphysics against skepticism.[4]

CHAPTER TWO

"Veil of Perception" Skepticism

PHILOSOPHERS in the Anglophone tradition tend to be in the habit of assuming that skepticism can be equated with, or at least has its paradigmatic form in, Berkeley's problem of a "veil of perception." Accordingly, many, if not most, Kant-interpreters in the Anglophone tradition write as though this problem were central to the critical philosophy.[1] However, such a picture of the critical philosophy seems to me fundamentally mistaken. Unlike the other two types of skepticism recently mentioned, "veil of perception" skepticism played no significant role in the origination of the critical philosophy, and no more than a secondary role in its mature motivation.[2]

Now there is, to be sure, some prima facie evidence to the contrary. In the *Critique* Kant famously makes no less than two efforts to answer "veil of perception" skepticism (which he there calls "skeptical" or "problematic idealism" and associates with Descartes),[3] one in the Fourth Paralogism of the first edition, the other in the second edition's Refutation of Idealism; and in the second edition he also describes the absence hitherto of a proper refutation of it as "a scandal to philosophy and to human reason."[4] Less famously, Kant had already shown an interest in, and a concern to respond to, this sort of skepticism at a very early period of his career. In his *New Elucidation* of 1755, an essay in precritical metaphysics which he wrote in the general spirit of his Rationalist predecessors, he derived from the principle of sufficient reason a "principle of succession" according to which no change or succession of states can occur in a substance except through interaction with another substance,[5] and then, towards the end of the essay, he made a special application of this "principle of succession" in order to defeat skepticism about the mind-external world, arguing that because of this principle changes in mental substances cannot occur "apart from a connection with other things [which] must be present outside the mind."[6] Nonetheless, to infer from these facts that "veil of perception" skepticism played a central role in either the origination or the mature motivation of the critical philosophy would, in my opinion, be a mistake.

To sketch a case, first, for denying that it played any significant role in the critical philosophy's *origination*: A first and fundamental point to note here is that, after Kant's brief concern with it in the *New Elucidation* of 1755, this sort of skepticism played hardly any part in the voluminous body of writings, letters, and private notes which preceded and prepared the ground for the *Critique* of 1781.[7] During this period Kant's considered view of skepticism concerning the external world seems to have been that empirical judgments about the external world are on the whole so certain that it is simply not a position worth taking seriously.[8] (Accordingly, even in the first edition of the *Critique* from 1781 Kant's explicit concern with this sort of skepticism is confined to an obscure corner, the Fourth Paralogism, only achieving any prominence in the *second* edition of 1787, where he first introduces the Refutation of Idealism and his "scandal" remarks.)

Nor should one be misled—as many Anglophone interpreters have been—by Kant's famous report in the preface of the *Prolegomena* that the aim of answering Hume's skeptical problems concerning causation was pivotal for his own original development of the critical philosophy.[9] Commentators in the Anglophone tradition have often assumed that this shows that answering "veil of perception" skepticism must have been one of the original and fundamental motives behind the critical philosophy.[10] Now Hume *had* in fact articulated a form of "veil of perception" skepticism, indeed even in a work available to Kant in translation from an early period, namely *An Enquiry concern-*

ing the Human Understanding (henceforth: *Enquiry*),[11] albeit briefly, towards the end of the work, and alongside numerous other skeptical ideas contained in the work, so Kant *could* reasonably have thought of Hume as a "veil of perception" skeptic. But the fact remains that he pretty clearly *did not*. Thus (as we shall see in detail later), the Humean skeptical problems concerning causation to which Kant is referring in the *Prolegomena* are conceptually quite distinct from "veil of perception" skepticism, and are understood by Kant as such. Moreover, Kant *nowhere* associates Hume with "veil of perception" skepticism. On the contrary, at least in the critical period, he normally thinks of Hume as a commonsense realist about the mind-external world.[12]

Turning to the question of the role of "veil of perception" skepticism in the *mature motivation* of the critical philosophy: Aside from the Fourth Paralogism and the Refutation of Idealism, where else in the main body of the *Critique* does a concern to address this sort of skepticism play a significant role? The correct answer, I think, is "Nowhere." In particular, various features of the text which have commonly tempted Anglophone interpreters into supposing otherwise—for example, a pervasive strategy of defending controversial concepts and principles by showing them to be conditions of the possibility of *experience* (*Erfahrung*); the central role assigned in the Transcendental Deduction to the principle of the "transcendental unity of apperception," or the necessary *self-ascribability of all one's representations*; and the central role played in the Analogies of Experience by a distinction between the temporal order of one's *subjective representations* and the temporal order of objective events—turn out, once properly interpreted, to constitute no evidence at all of a concern on Kant's part to take this sort of skepticism into account. Demonstrating this properly from the texts would take some time, but here are a few hints. (1) It is important to realize that when Kant pursues his pervasive strategy of showing controversial concepts and principles to be conditions of the possibility of *experience*, he normally means by this term, not merely subjective representations of a sort that a "veil of perception" skeptic would concede, but *empirical knowl-*

edge of objects: "Experience is an empirical cognition [*Erkenntnis*], that is, a cognition which determines an object through perceptions."[13] (2) In the Transcendental Deduction his approach is to demonstrate that the a priori concepts of the understanding have application by showing their application to be a necessary condition for fulfillment of the principle of the "transcendental unity of apperception," or the necessary self-ascribability of all one's representations. Now this principle certainly looks as though it *could in fact* withstand "veil of perception" skepticism. But that does not prove that Kant selected it *because* it could withstand "veil of perception" skepticism. He might instead have done so for the entirely different reason that it is in its turn a necessary condition of one's having any knowledge at all, including in particular empirical knowledge of external objects (since knowing requires having representations).[14] And in fact the text makes it clear that he *is* allowing himself an assumption that we have knowledge of the latter weighty sort.[15] So, actually, this alternative explanation of his focus on the principle seems clearly to be the correct one. (3) In the Second Analogy Kant's strategy is to prove the principle that every event has a cause by showing the application of this principle to be a necessary condition of one's in certain cases having knowledge that a temporal sequence in one's representations is not merely subjective but reflects an objective event.[16] But this strategy simply *assumes* that we *do* in certain cases have such objective knowledge.

What, then, should we make of Kant's early concern with "veil of perception" skepticism in the *New Elucidation* of 1755 and the *Critique*'s concern with it in the Fourth Paralogism of the first edition and the Refutation of Idealism and "scandal" remarks of the second edition?

In the case of the *New Elucidation* it is clear both from the essay's internal course and from Kant's surrounding writings that the essay's main motives concerned metaphysical questions which had nothing to do with "veil of perception" skepticism; that Kant found, however, that those motives led to a metaphysical position, namely the "principle of succession," which yielded the possibility of refuting "veil of perception" skepticism as a sort of happy by-product; and that he therefore decided to exploit this possibility toward the end of the essay as an addendum to its central business.

The points made above regarding the absence of any significant concern with "veil of perception" skepticism in the period and process leading up to the *Critique*, and its absence from the motivation of the central parts of the work, strongly suggest a similar picture of the role of "veil of perception" skepticism in the *Critique*: Having originally developed the critical philosophy in response to a set of concerns which had nothing to do with "veil of perception" skepticism (as in the *New Elucidation*, largely concerns about metaphysics), Kant found that these had led him to a position which offered the possibility of answering "veil of perception" skepticism as a sort of happy by-product—specifically, in the first edition, a qualified form of phenomenalism arrived at in that edition's Transcendental Deduction as part of its solution to the problem of how a priori concepts can refer to objects, which Kant subsequently reinvokes in the Fourth Paralogism in order to refute "veil of perception" skepticism; and in the second edition, the First Analogy's principle that time-determination requires a knowledge of substances, which he subsequently reinvokes in the Refutation of Idealism in application to the time-determination of subjective states in order to refute "veil of perception" skepticism. He therefore chose to exploit these opportunities as an addendum to his central project.

This interpretation of the role of "veil of perception" skepticism in the *Critique* is confirmed by two obvious features of the parts of the work which explicitly address this sort of skepticism. First, they appear to be "tacked on" to the main body of the work. Thus, after the first three Paralogisms have been uniformly concerned with exposing fallacies in rational psychology's inferences from characteristics of the formal "I think" to doctrines about the nature of a substantive soul, the Fourth Paralogism's concern with addressing "veil of perception" skepticism looks like a very odd man out. And in the case of the Refutation of Idealism, not only does its sandwiching into the Postulates of Empirical Thought, with their focus on the modal categories of possibility, actuality, and necessity, give it the same appearance, but of course this time we *know* that this is due to its having been tacked on. Second, these parts of the *Critique* exhibit extraordinary instability. Having in the first edition pursued one line of argument against "veil of perception" skepticism in the Fourth Paralogism, Kant scraps it and substitutes an entirely different one in the second edition's Refutation of Idealism, and then tries a number of variations on the latter, already beginning in the preface,[17] and subsequently in his private notes.[18] This again strongly suggests that the material has the character of late afterthoughts added to the main body of the work.

Someone might, I suppose, reply that, even granting that the *Critique*'s interest in "veil of perception" skepticism emerged in the way just indicated and with the limited reach in the work just indicated, still the work should be seen as belatedly admitting it to the circle of its central motives, and as not so much disregarding it in such core sections as the Transcendental Deduction and the Analogies, as deferring its treatment to the section which explicitly deals with it (the Fourth Paralogism or the Refutation of Idealism). However, I am skeptical. Such an argument certainly seems far-fetched in relation to the first-edition *Critique*. For example, why in that case does "veil of perception" skepticism play hardly any role in the *Prolegomena* of 1783?[19] The argument seems slightly more persuasive in relation to the second-edition *Critique*—due to Kant's prominent "scandal" remarks in the preface and his substitution of the more prominent Refutation of Idealism for the obscure Fourth Paralogism. But, even in connection with the second edition, is it not more plausible to ascribe the new prominence of "veil of perception" skepticism to an author's natural tendency to emphasize his latest material? Certainly, Kant's numerous subsequent pronouncements concerning the *Critique* and its subject matter—in letters, private notes, lectures (especially those on metaphysics), and formal writings (especially *On a Discovery* from 1790 and the *Prize Essay on Progress in Metaphysics* of 1791)—lend no support at all to the idea that "veil of perception" skepticism ever became more than a secondary concern for him.[20]

Now, of course, someone might concede these interpretive points but still want to argue that "veil of perception" skepticism deserves a prominent place in any discussion of the critical philosophy for reasons *other than* its centrality to the genesis and motivation of the critical philosophy. In particular, it might be argued that it does so because it is a skeptical problem of great intrinsic philosophical importance, or because Kant's answer to it is unusually compelling, or both. However, I do not believe that this problem *is* nearly as important as it has often been taken to be. One reason why not is that it essentially rests on an assumption which itself turns out to be vulnerable to skepticism, namely an assumption that, unlike one's beliefs about the mind-external world, one's beliefs about one's own subjective mental states are certain (I shall return to this topic, albeit from a slightly different angle, in chapter 12).[21] Nor would I agree that Kant's answer to it *is* unusually compelling. On the contrary, the Fourth Paralogism and the Refutation of Idealism seem to me among the weakest parts of the *Critique*.[22]

In sum, Kant's supposed deep preoccupation with "veil of perception" skepticism is more a figment of certain interpreters' imaginations than a reality—a sort of parallax produced by an idiosyncrasy in their own philosophical perspective.

CHAPTER THREE

Skepticism and Metaphysics (a Puzzle)

THE *CRITIQUE* is primarily a book about metaphysics (as can already be seen from the thematic focus of its two prefaces, for instance). Accordingly, the types of skepticism that *did* play a crucial role in the origination of the critical philosophy and that it *is* mainly concerned to address are instead certain types of skepticism which threaten metaphysics specifically.

What *was* "metaphysics" for Kant? The discipline's origins of course lay in Aristotle's *Metaphysics*, which had contained two different conceptions of it in uneasy combination with each other: a conception of it as a science of being as such (book gamma), and a conception of it as a science of those beings which have only form, not matter (book lambda).[1] After a long and complicated intervening history, the discipline had come to play a large role in German academia during the seventeenth and eighteenth centuries, taking a variety of forms.[2] For most of the Germans in question, and in particular for the Leibniz-inspired authors of the eighteenth century who immediately preceded Kant, including Wolff and Baumgarten, as well as for the precritical Kant himself until about 1765, the discipline comprised two parts, roughly corresponding to Aristotle's two original conceptions. First, there was "general metaphysics," or "general ontology." This gave an account of our most general concepts and principles, those that applied to all beings. Prominent examples were the concepts of substance and accident, and cause and effect, and the principle of sufficient reason. Second, there was "special metaphysics." This dealt with three supersensible beings: the world as a whole, the human soul, and God.[3]

In the *Critique* Kant famously gives an account of progress in relation to the discipline of metaphysics according to which the inquiry begins *dogmatically*, then turns *skeptical*, before finally becoming *critical*.[4] This account should be understood not only as history but also as *autobiography*.

Now we can approach the question of the specific *types* of skepticism concerning metaphysics which were crucial for the origination and motivation of Kant's critical philosophy via an exegetical puzzle. In two different places Kant gives two different and seemingly incompatible accounts of what originally woke him from the "slumber" of "dogmatic" metaphysics and set him on the path towards the critical philosophy. In the *Prolegomena* of 1783 he famously writes: "I openly confess: David Hume's reminder was the very thing which many years ago first interrupted my dogmatic slumber and gave my investigations in the field of speculative philosophy a quite new direction."[5] On the other hand, in a letter to Christian Garve from 1798 he states that it was the Antinomies that played this role: "The antinomy of pure reason—'The world has a beginning; it has no beginning, and so on,' right up to the fourth [*sic*]: 'There is freedom in man, versus there is no freedom, only the necessity of nature'—that is what first aroused me from my dogmatic slumber and drove me to the critique of reason itself, in order to resolve the scandal of ostensible contradiction of reason with itself."[6]

Faced with the apparent inconsistency between these two passages, one commentator (Lewis White Beck) in effect resorts to the hypothesis that in the latter passage Kant is senile![7] However, this explanation is surely desperate and implausible. For one thing, Kant had already made essentially the same point as he makes in the latter passage in the earlier and more formal context of his *Prize Essay on Progress in Metaphysics* of 1791 (henceforth: *Prize Essay*).[8]

The *proper* explanation is more complicated and interesting: Both passages contain a large and important measure of truth.

They refer to two different, but equally significant, historical steps which Kant took in his protracted escape from the clutches of dogmatic metaphysics towards the (supposed) safe haven of the critical philosophy. Each step consisted in his recognition of, and reaction to, a kind of skepticism which he saw confronting dogmatic metaphysics, though the kinds of skepticism involved in the two cases were very different. The letter to Garve refers to an encounter with Pyrrhonian equipollence skepticism which occurred in the mid-1760s, whereas the passage from the *Prolegomena* refers mainly to an encounter with Humean skepticism concerning the possibility of a priori concepts and synthetic a priori knowledge which occurred either in or shortly after 1772. Let me explain, beginning with the earlier encounter alluded to by the letter to Garve.

Chapter Four

Kant's Pyrrhonian Crisis

THE LETTER to Garve is alluding to a *crise pyrrhonienne*, in the strict sense of a skeptical crisis based on the principles of the ancient Pyrrhonists, which came to dominate Kant's attitude to the discipline of metaphysics in the mid-1760s.

The allusion is slightly inaccurate, or at least misleading, in that it suggests that Kant's original escape from dogmatic metaphysics was due to the impulse of precisely the four Antinomies expounded in the *Critique*. A more careful formulation would rather have said (1) that it was due to the impulse of a family of problems which shared the same general structure and subject matter as the Antinomies of the *Critique*, and (2) that these included, but were not restricted to, early versions of the four Antinomies of the *Critique*. Very modestly revised in this way, however, the testimony of the letter concerning the stimulus that first roused Kant from the "slumber" of "dogmatic" metaphysics can be confirmed, and its impact moreover dated to about the year 1765.

Thus, concerning, first, point (1): The *general structure* of the *Critique*'s Antinomies is one of setting pairs of contrary (or apparently contrary) propositions into opposition to each other and furnishing each of them with supporting arguments of equal strength.[1] Their *general subject matter* is the set of supersensible entities that had been treated by traditional "special metaphysics": the world as a whole, the human soul, and God.[2] Now the letter's implication that problems of this general type motivated Kant's original disaffection with traditional metaphysics and moved him towards the critical philosophy is confirmed, and the date of this process moreover fixed to about 1765, by another letter which Kant wrote, this time a letter to Bernouilli from 1781 (the year of the *Critique*'s first publication). For in this letter to Bernouilli Kant identifies problems having just the general structure and subject matter in question as the original source of his ambition to reform the discipline of metaphysics, and he makes it clear that this stimulus was already at work on him in the year 1765. Discussing his correspondence with the recently deceased Lambert, Kant refers in his 1781 letter to a proposal which Lambert had made to him at the end of Lambert's first letter to him of November 13, 1765 that they—in Kant's words—"collaborate on the reform of metaphysics," and Kant goes on to say:

> *I saw at that time* [i.e., late 1765] *that this putative science lacked a touchstone with which to distinguish truth from deception, since different but equally persuasive metaphysical propositions lead inescapably to contradictory conclusions, with the result that one proposition inevitably casts doubt on the other.* I had some ideas for a possible reform of this science then, but I wanted my ideas to mature first before submitting them to my friend's penetrating scrutiny.[3]

Concerning, next, point (2): On the one hand, early versions of the *Critique*'s four Antinomies were indeed already known, and of concern, to Kant by the year 1765.[4] But on the other hand, Kant had not yet in 1765 brought the Antinomies together into any such canonical system of four as they constitute in the *Critique*.[5] And in this early period he was also concerned with further "antinomies" over and above those four.[6] So the stimulus at work in 1765 included but was *not restricted to* early versions of the four Antinomies of the *Critique*.

I said that this crisis which Kant saw confronting metaphysics in the mid-1760s was *Pyrrhonian*. This is true in two senses. First, it was Pyrrhonian in *character*. Specifically, it was so both in virtue of the general *structure* of the problems which it raised against metaphysical claims, namely a setting of each claim against a contrary claim and demonstration that equally strong arguments could be given on both sides (as Kant puts it in his letter to Bernouilli, "different but equally persuasive metaphys-

ical propositions lead inescapably to contrary conclusions"),
and in virtue of the immediate *result* of those problems, namely
a suspension of judgment about the issues in question (as Kant
puts it in the same letter, "one proposition inevitably casts
doubt on the other"). For this is precisely an example of ancient ·
Pyrrhonism's procedure of establishing *isostheneia*, or "equipollence" (lit. "equal force on both sides"), with the result of pro-
ducing *epochê*, or "suspension of judgment"—a procedure which
Sextus Empiricus, the main spokesman of ancient Pyrrhonism,
describes (and then richly illustrates with examples) as "the
main basic principle of the skeptic system."[7] (Notice that the
Critique itself identifies this as the classic procedure of skepticism: "A skeptical objection sets assertion and counter-assertion
in mutual opposition to each other as having equal weight . . .
And the conflict is taken as showing that all judgment in regard
to the object is completely null and void."[8])

Second, the crisis of the mid-1760s was also largely Pyrrhonian in *inspiration*. Evidence for this can be found in a short text
from the period, *Notice concerning the Structure of Lectures in the
Winter Semester 1765–1766* (henceforth: *Notice*). In this text
Kant expresses skepticism about existing metaphysics (in sharp
contrast to mathematics, history, natural science, etc.), arguing
that it constitutes merely "an illusion of science . . . which is
regarded as the real thing only at a particular place and among
particular people but which is everywhere else despised." And
he goes on to say that "the special method of instruction in
[metaphysical] philosophy is *zetetic*, as some ancients called it
(from *zêtein*), that is to say *investigative*."[9] Now by a "zetetic"
method Kant can here mean only one thing: *the Pyrrhonists'
equipollence method, or procedure of balancing opposed arguments in
order to produce a suspension of judgment.*[10]

The *Notice* from 1765 did not yet represent Kant's metaphysical *crise pyrrhonienne* in full bloom, though.[11] That came shortly
afterwards in his 1766 essay *Dreams of a Spirit Seer, Illustrated
by Dreams of Metaphysics* (henceforth: *Dreams of a Spirit Seer*).
Following his decision to apply the zetetic, or equipollence,
method to metaphysics in a systematic way had by now led him
to the conclusion that the promise of knowledge about the su-

persensible which had hitherto been the discipline's main claim
to fame was a hollow one.[12] He therefore now advocated the
abandonment of supersensuous metaphysics as a spurious discipline, and bade his readers instead resist its temptations and
confine themselves to "the lowly ground of experience and the
common understanding."[13] By this, he made clear in the essay,
he meant more specifically empirical, mathematical, moral, and
logical cognition.[14] He did salvage for "metaphysics" the task
of serving as a "science of the bounds of human reason" which
ensures that our judgments are based on "empirical concepts
. . . upon which all our judgments must at all times rest."[15]
However, this really just amounted to putting a new discipline
under the old name.[16]

Indeed (a point which is easily overlooked), Kant in *Dreams
of a Spirit Seer* embraced what he must himself have considered
a pretty strict form of Pyrrhonism.[17] For, not only is the zetetic
method which underlies the work's rejection of supersensuous
metaphysics Pyrrhonian in both character and inspiration (as
we have seen), but in addition, the work's estimation of which
types of cognition fall victim to this method and which do not
is precisely that of Pyrrhonism as Kant interprets it.[18] This can
be seen from his extended and enthusiastic treatment of Pyrrhonism in his early logic lectures, especially the *Blomberg Logic*
of 1771, where he interprets Pyrrho's position as one which—
exactly like his own in *Dreams of a Spirit Seer*—does not in general attack empirical, mathematical, moral, or logical judgments, but instead just the judgments of supersensuous metaphysics.[19] In addition, the prominence in *Dreams of a Spirit Seer*
of the ideals of the *useful*, *happiness*, and everyday *life*[20] points
unmistakably to a strong *normative* agreement with Pyrrhonism, for which each of these concepts likewise functioned as a
prominent normative ideal.

In sum, *Dreams of a Spirit Seer* of 1766 represents a *crise pyrrhonienne* in full bloom, and is indeed to all intents and purposes
a self-consciously Pyrrhonian work.[21]

Kant's position from the mid-1760s that, unlike other disciplines, traditional metaphysics, in transcending experience, falls
victim to the Pyrrhonian problem of equally balanced opposing

arguments, and therefore requires some sort of radical reform, survives to hold a prominent place in the critical philosophy's explanation of the motives behind its own reform of metaphysics. For example, the first edition of the *Critique* famously opens with a lament that in resorting to principles which "overstep all possible empirical employment . . . human reason precipitates itself into darkness and contradictions; and while it may indeed conjecture that these must be in some way due to concealed errors, it is not in a position to be able to detect them. For since the principles of which it is making use transcend the limits of experience, they are no longer subject to any empirical test. The battlefield of these endless controversies is called metaphysics."[22] And the *Prolegomena* contrasts traditional metaphysics with other sciences which "obtain universal and permanent recognition," noting that "in all ages one metaphysics has contradicted another, either in its assertions or their proofs, and thus has itself destroyed its claim to lasting assent. Indeed, the attempts to set up such a science were without doubt the primary cause of skepticism's so early appearance."[23]

Clearly, in such passages from the critical period Kant is largely thinking of the canonical four Antinomies of the *Critique*.[24] Someone might indeed propose that that is *all* he is thinking of.[25] However, the passages' general tenor surely also suggests a *broader* concern with equipollence problems afflicting supersensuous metaphysics. And this impression is reinforced by two further facts: First, within the *Critique* itself Kant mentions a number of additional areas of metaphysics in which equipollence problems pose a threat.[26] Second, he not only *preceded* the critical philosophy with such broader concerns (as we have seen), but also *explicitly returned* to them after the *Critique*, adding in the *Critique of Practical Reason*, the *Critique of Judgment*, and *Religion within the Limits of Reason Alone* further "antinomies" over and above the canonical four.[27] So I would suggest that in the critical philosophy Kant is in fact still very much concerned with Pyrrhonian equipollence problems afflicting supersensuous metaphysics in a way that not only includes but also extends beyond the canonical four Antinomies.

CHAPTER FIVE

Humean Skepticism

LET US NOW CONSIDER the other skeptical impulse which, according to Kant, this time in the *Prolegomena*, awoke him from his dogmatic metaphysical slumber and gave his philosophy a new direction: "David Hume's reminder." The general nature of this reminder is clear enough from the *Prolegomena*: Hume's skeptical reflections concerning causation. It is much less clear, though, exactly what it was in Hume's rather various skeptical reflections on causation that awoke Kant, when it did so, and how it did so. Let me therefore attempt to answer those questions.

Close examination of the *Prolegomena*—and of a corresponding discussion of Hume in the *Critique*[1]—reveals that, although Kant does not distinguish between them very clearly, he in fact has three quite distinct Humean views concerning causation in mind. First, he has in mind Hume's argument that particular causal connections and laws cannot be known a priori by reason alone but only from experience, since their denial is never self-contradictory or inconceivable in the way that is required for a priori knowledge to be possible.[2] Second, he has in mind Hume's position that the component idea of necessity which is contained in the idea of a cause must be traceable, like all other ideas, to a corresponding antecedent impression, and that the search for such an impression reveals causal necessity to consist, not in a property of causally related items themselves, but instead in what Hume describes as the "customary transition of the imagination from one object to its usual attendant" in the subject's thought.[3] Third, he has in mind Hume's view that the principle that every event has a cause (henceforth: the causal principle) can only be known "from observation and experience," since (once again) its denial is not self-contradictory or inconceivable in the way required for a priori knowledge to be possible.[4]

The first of these Humean views seems to have exerted an influence on Kant by the mid-1760s at the latest, when Kant embraced it wholeheartedly in *Dreams of a Spirit Seer* (1766).[5] Kant notes in the same work and in a letter to Mendelssohn from the same period that this principle concerning the knowledge of particular causal connections and laws carries strong negative consequences for traditional metaphysics' claims to knowledge of the supersensible, because it rules out as illegitimate any claim to know about the causation of items of experience by supersensible items, or vice versa, or about causal relations between supersensible items themselves.[6] The first part of this point (the exclusion of claims to know about the causation of items of experience by supersensible items) was especially important, because it precluded any metaphysics that, like Kant's own before the period in question,[7] presumed to infer from items of experience to supersensible items as their explanatorily required causes. This, then, was evidently Kant's first significant debt to Hume.[8]

However, this first Humean view is clearly not what Kant *mainly* has in mind in the *Prolegomena* as the influence that awoke him from his dogmatic slumber in metaphysics. This can be seen from three related facts. First, Kant says that the Humean views which roused him were ones which only presented him with a problem to solve but that he "was far from following [Hume] in the conclusions to which he arrived."[9] But this does not characterize Kant's attitude to the first Humean view, whose point he simply *accepted* in the 1760s,[10] and continued to accept in the critical philosophy;[11] and whose negative implication for causal inferences from experience to the supersensible he likewise accepted permanently.[12] It does, on the other hand, characterize his attitude to the other two Humean views, those concerned with causal necessity and the causal principle. Second, the answers to Humean problems which Kant goes on to sketch in the *Prolegomena* are answers, not to the first Humean view, but rather to these other two Humean views—namely, in the preface, the Metaphysical/Transcendental Deduction of the a priori concepts of the understanding (including the concept of cause or causal necessity),[13] and, in sections 27–30, the Analogies of Experience (which seek to prove the causal principle, among other principles). Third, a passage from the *Critique* identifies Hume's commitment to these other two views as constituting the skepticism that produces the transition from dogmatism in metaphysics to criticism.[14] It is therefore on these other two Humean views that we should mainly focus.

In order to see when and how these other two Humean views impinged on Kant's development, we need to return to the writings of the precritical Kant. Four years after publishing *Dreams of a Spirit Seer* in 1766 Kant went on to publish the *Inaugural Dissertation* of 1770. In many respects this work marked a huge advance beyond *Dreams of a Spirit Seer* towards the critical philosophy. In particular, Kant now for the first time sharply distinguished the faculties of sensibility and intellect (or understanding), developed the phenomena-noumena distinction, and, above all, advanced the theory that space and time, as pure intuitions and pure forms of sensible intuition, are merely ideal—all in ways which would require little modification in the *Critique*. However, in another respect the *Inaugural Dissertation* represented a major slide backwards. For Kant was once again indulging in the sweet slumber of supersensuous metaphysics. Thus according to the *Inaugural Dissertation* the intellect furnishes us with a knowledge of noumena or "things which cannot by their own nature come before the senses of the subject," including in particular God.[15] If Kant's letter to Garve alludes to his awakening by Pyrrhonian skepticism from the long metaphysical sleep that ended in the mid-1760s, his remarks on Hume's reminder in the *Prolegomena* allude mainly to his awakening by Humean skepticism from this briefer metaphysical snooze in the *Inaugural Dissertation*.

The initial impetus behind this second awakening seems in fact to have come from Kant himself rather than from Hume, however (in crediting Hume he errs on the side of generosity). In a famous letter which he wrote to Herz in 1772 Kant has two second thoughts about a supersensuous metaphysics of the sort that he had adopted in the *Inaugural Dissertation*.[16] First, he has a worry concerning the ability of concepts to refer to supersensible objects in the manner envisaged by the *Inaugural Dissertation*. His worry is as follows: It is clear enough, he argues, that a concept can refer to an object if the object is the cause of the concept, as in the case of concepts belonging to sensibility (sensibility having been *defined* in the *Inaugural Dissertation* as the capacity of the subject to be affected by the presence of an object).[17] It is also clear enough that a concept can refer to an object if the concept is the cause of the object—as would notionally be the case for concepts which belonged to a divine archetypal intellect. But since the intellect's concepts of supersensible noumena as envisaged by the *Inaugural Dissertation* refer in *neither* of these two ways, it is unclear how they can refer at all, as the *Inaugural Dissertation* supposed they did.[18] Second, he has an additional worry concerning the possibility of *knowing* about supersensible noumena in the manner envisaged by the *Inaugural Dissertation*. His concern this time is the very simple one that (over and above problems about reference) it is unclear how one could have a knowledge of things not attained through experience of them.[19]

The two remaining Humean views concerning causation correspond closely to these two worries about metaphysics, and seem to have contributed to Kant's development away from the metaphysics of the *Inaugural Dissertation* some time shortly after Kant wrote to Herz in 1772. As many commentators have argued, it is likely that the publication in 1772 of Beattie's *An Essay on the Nature and Immutability of Truth* in a German translation played an important role here, because this for the first time made Hume's view concerning the causal principle accessible to Kant.[20]

The exact role played by the two Humean views in the development of Kant's thought is by no means easy to determine from the scant evidence available. But it seems in both cases to have had two sides in tension with each other: On the one hand, the *general principles* which lay behind these Humean views suggested to Kant more refined ways of reformulating the two prima facie objections which he had already himself raised against supersensuous metaphysics in the letter to Herz. On the other hand, and in tension with that, the *specific subject matters* of Hume's views—the concept of causal necessity and the causal principle—furnished Kant with especially instructive test cases for the (now refined) prima facie objections, suggesting that there had, in fact, to be something wrong with them, and thus pointing the way towards a metaphysics which might survive their attack. Let me now develop this interpretation in a little more detail.

Consider first Hume's analysis of the concept of causal necessity. The general principle which drove Hume to give this analysis was the principle that every idea requires a corresponding antecedent impression as its source. Kant had in fact long been familiar with such a position.[21] Moreover, he had himself long found it tempting, although never accepting it unequivocally.[22] Hume's principle seems to have reminded Kant of this position, and to have thereby alerted him to the possibility of a more radical version of his own worry in the letter to Herz concerning the concepts of supersensuous metaphysics. Setting aside the merely notional theological case of concepts which cause their objects, Kant's own worry in the letter had basically been that concepts not derived from sensibility and thereby causally dependent on their objects could not refer. Now Hume with his "No impression, no idea" principle had gone one step further than that: concepts not derived from sensible antecedents could certainly not refer because they could not even *exist*. It appears that Kant found Hume's principle sufficiently plausible to take this more radical worry about the concepts of supersensuous metaphysics seriously in addition to his own original worry.[23] Accordingly, these two worries would later *together* constitute the fundamental problematic of the Metaphysical and Transcendental Deductions in the *Critique*. For example, both are in Kant's mind at the very start of the Transcendental

Deduction, where he first says that the problem involved is whether a priori concepts have "a meaning, an imagined significance" (i.e., the more radical Humean worry),[24] and then that it is how they can "relate to objects which they yet do not obtain from any experience" (i.e., Kant's own original worry).[25]

To say that Kant found Hume's "No impression, no idea" principle and the radical worry about the very existence of the concepts of supersensuous metaphysics which flowed from it plausible is not, however, to say that he ultimately accepted them.[26] Indeed, I suggest that one reason why he found Hume's application of the principle to the particular concept of causal necessity so enlightening was precisely that this application afforded a sort of prima facie reduction to absurdity of the principle: Thanks largely to the relative perspicuity of this particular concept's existence and character, the application of the principle to it could be clearly seen to lead unavoidably to a conclusion that was false—namely, Hume's conclusion that the concept of causal necessity, if it exists at all, expresses, not a relation between causally related items themselves, but instead merely the mind's reaction to constant conjunction. As Kant saw things, the concept clearly did exist, but it equally clearly did not express *that*. Therefore the Humean principle had to be false.[27]

A second reason why Kant found Hume's example enlightening, I suggest, is that he drew from it similar instruction concerning his own original, less radical worry about the ability of concepts lacking sensible antecedents to refer. Hume's examination of the concept of cause, once corrected by Kant so as to excise what he considered to be its manifestly mistaken derivation of the essential component concept of necessity from a subjective impression, had shown it to be a concept containing an essential component concept not derivable from sensible antecedents.[28] Yet it must have seemed clear to Kant on reflection that the concepts of cause in general and causal necessity in particular nevertheless do succeed in referring, since, despite their failure to be derivable without remainder from sensation, they are found to be instantiated in experience in a broader, everyday sense of "experience" (after all, we do in *some* sense see rocks causing windows to break, etc.), and are moreover indispensable to the outlooks of common sense and natural science alike.[29] Consequently, Kant's own original worry that concepts could only refer insofar as they were derived from sensible antecedents now looked as though it had to be mistaken.

To put these two points in another way: As long as one had focused on such hazy, lofty, and dispensable metaphysical terms as, for example, "God," Hume's radical worry and Kant's own original worry had looked quite plausible. Perhaps such terms really *did* lack meaning or at least reference.[30] But once one realized that the same two worries would apply, if at all, just as much to such seemingly perspicuous, experiential, and indispensable concepts as "cause" as well, it was rather the *worries* that came to look misconceived.

Consider next the other relevant Humean position concerning causation alluded to by the *Prolegomena*: knowledge of the causal principle must be based on experience, since its denial is not self-contradictory or inconceivable in the way required for a priori knowledge to be possible. Once again, this position seems to have played two roles in Kant's development in tension with each other, this time in relation to the prima facie objection already raised by Kant himself against supersensuous metaphysics that it is unclear how the intellect could achieve knowledge concerning things of which it has no experience. On the one hand, the general doctrine behind Hume's position suggested to Kant a more cogent reformulation of his own prima facie objection. On the other hand, the specific subject matter of Hume's position, the causal principle, provided a particularly instructive test case for the now-refined prima facie objection, suggesting that there had in fact to be something wrong with it.

The general doctrine that lay behind Hume's position on the causal principle was what has come to be known as Hume's "fork," long familiar to Kant in the form that Hume had given it in the *Enquiry*. As articulated in the *Enquiry*, the "fork" consisted of the following three claims. First, all known truths are divisible into two kinds: on the one hand, "relations of ideas," defined by Hume as propositions "intuitively or demonstratively certain," by which he seems to mean such that their deni-

als either are or imply contradictions; on the other hand, "matters of fact," defined as all the rest. Second, while relations of
ideas "are discoverable by the mere operation of thought," or
in other words a priori, matters of fact are only knowable by
means of experience, or a posteriori—since, beyond present
sensory experience and memories of past sensory experience,
only causal reasoning can furnish us with this kind of knowledge, and it turns out that causal insight itself "arises entirely
from experience."[31] Third, and consequently, if it is found that
a proposition—Hume adds with feigned casualness, "of divinity
or school metaphysics for instance"—is neither certain by virtue of its denial being or implying a contradiction nor known
by means of experience, then we may "commit it . . . to the
flames: for it can contain nothing but sophistry and illusion."[32]
Since it seemed clear to Hume that the causal principle was not
known by virtue of its denial being or implying a contradiction,
his only option, short of rejecting it as altogether "sophistry and
illusion," was to say that it was known by means of experience.[33]

How did Hume's "fork" enable Kant to reformulate in a
more cogent fashion his own prima facie objection to supersensuous metaphysics from the letter to Herz, namely the objection that it is unclear how the intellect could achieve knowledge
concerning things of which it has no experience? The "fork"
shared with this Kantian objection an assumption that a posteriori knowledge of things is, generally speaking, philosophically
unproblematic. But the "fork" also made explicit, and evidently
alerted Kant to, something that his own objection had overlooked, namely the fact that there is in addition a substantial
and well-defined class of *a priori* cognitions which are unproblematic: those that are true simply in virtue of the law of contradiction (in Hume's terminology, relations of ideas; in Kant's,
analytic judgments).[34] Kant of course readily took this important qualification to heart.[35] In this way the "fork" enabled
him to formulate a more refined version of his own original
objection to supersensuous metaphysics. The objection was
now no longer that it was unclear how there could be a priori
knowledge *generally*, but instead that it was unclear how there
could be a priori knowledge which did not belong to the un-

problematic class founded on the law of contradiction (in Kant's terminology: a priori knowledge which was not "analytic" but "synthetic"). This objection, already in effect advanced by Hume as the thrust of his "fork," now reappears as the central puzzle of the *Critique*, on the settlement of which, according to the work itself, the very fate of metaphysics depends: "How are a priori synthetic judgments possible?"[36]

In tension with this influence exerted by its underlying general principle, the "fork," however, Hume's position concerning the causal principle was also important for Kant because the causal principle, specifically, provided him with an illuminating test case for the now-refined objection to supersensuous metaphysics (in effect, the objection that there is no such thing as synthetic a priori knowledge). Kant agreed with Hume that the causal principle was a clear case of genuine knowledge—for it was supported by confirming instances in experience, and was moreover fundamental to the outlooks of common sense and natural science alike.[37] He also agreed with Hume that the principle was obviously synthetic. However, the conclusion to which Hume had been unavoidably driven when he had applied his denial of synthetic a priori knowledge to the principle, namely that the principle was not known a priori but only a posteriori, seemed to Kant to be clearly false—especially because of the strict universality pertaining to the principle.[38] Consequently, scrutiny of the example of the causal principle afforded, in Kant's view, a strong prima facie disproof, or reduction to absurdity, of the denial that there could be synthetic a priori knowledge.[39]

To put the point in another way: As long as one had focused on such lofty and questionable synthetic a priori claims as, for example, that God had such and such characteristics or performed such and such acts, then the worry that synthetic a priori knowledge was impossible had looked plausible. Perhaps one *could not* know anything of that sort. But once one realized that this worry, if it applied at all, equally challenged such empirically confirmed and fundamental convictions as our conviction in the causal principle, then it was the *worry* that came to look misconceived.

In short, the two Humean skeptical views about causation enabled Kant both to refine the objections to supersensuous metaphysics which he had himself articulated in the letter to Herz and to show that, even so refined, there seemed in fact to be something wrong with them, so that the prospects for metaphysics were after all brighter than they had implied.

The latter side of this twofold process is reminiscent of a strategy that is characteristic of the Scottish common sense school: when a philosopher like Hume advances a philosophical principle which entails a deeply counterintuitive consequence, one holds fast to the intuitive position that is under attack and converts his modus ponendo ponens argument against that position into a modus tollendo tollens argument against his principle (i.e., one converts his "If p then q, p therefore q" into "If p then q, -q therefore -p"). Beattie in particular uses this strategy, and I suspect that he influenced Kant here (in other words, I suspect that his influence on Kant went beyond merely providing him with information about Hume's position on the causal principle, that it also had this more philosophical dimension). This might seem unlikely in view of Kant's sharp defense of Hume against the Scottish common sense school in the *Prolegomena*.[40] However, in its support, consider, for example, Kant's remark in his 1799 open letter on Fichte's *Wissenschaftslehre* that "the *Critique* . . . is to be understood exclusively from the point of view of common sense [*des gemeinen . . . Verstandes*]."[41] Kant's line of thought thus includes what could be called a *common sense moment*.

However, unlike the common sense school, Kant conceived this as only a prima facie response still in need of reinforcement and elaboration (this, I take it, is the *real* reason behind his defense of Hume against the common sense school in the *Prolegomena*). Until Hume's tempting principle "No impression, no idea" and Kant's own original tempting principle that (in effect) concepts can only refer insofar as they are derived from sensibility had received a more decisive and thorough refutation than this sort of appeal to particular counterintuitive consequences could constitute, they continued to represent a puzzle about the status of the concept of cause and other a priori concepts (an a priori concept being for Kant by definition one that fails to conform to Hume's principle, one that is not derivable from sensation, at least not without remainder).[42] This puzzle bore both a stick and a carrot for the discipline of metaphysics. The *stick* was that until the principles were more decisively and thoroughly refuted they still in some, even if diminished, degree threatened the claims of a priori concepts to exist and refer, and hence also the standing of metaphysics. After all, proponents of the principles in question might just bite the bullet in the face of the commonsense response and insist that the counterintuitive consequences flowing from them for such terms as "cause," and hence for common sense and science, simply must be correct. The *carrot* was the prospect that a more satisfactory solution to the puzzle might, in addition to dispelling this residual threat, afford new insights into such a priori concepts and into disciplines like metaphysics which depended upon them.

Similarly, until the tempting denial that there could be synthetic a priori knowledge had been given a more decisive and thorough refutation than this sort of appeal to particular counterintuitive consequences could constitute, it continued to represent a puzzle concerning the status of the causal principle and other apparently synthetic a priori principles. And, once again, the puzzle bore both a stick and a carrot. The *stick* was that, until more cogently answered, it continued to cast at least some doubt on the claims of synthetic a priori principles to constitute knowledge, and hence on disciplines such as metaphysics which relied on them. After all, as in the conceptual case, the philosopher who denied that there could be synthetic a priori knowledge might just bite the bullet and accept the particular counterintuitive consequences involved.[43] The *carrot* was that a full solution to the puzzle might afford new insights into principles of this kind and into disciplines such as metaphysics which relied on them.

In sum, I suggest that Kant's reflections in or shortly after 1772 on Hume's treatments of the concept of causal necessity and the causal principle in these ways brought him to a deeper (though not yet final) understanding than he had achieved alone in his letter to Herz of two major puzzles bearing on the possibility of metaphysics: a double puzzle about the existence and reference of a priori concepts, and a puzzle about the possibility of synthetic a priori knowledge. It is mainly this process that Kant has in mind in the *Prolegomena* when he credits Hume with having roused him from the slumber of dogmatic metaphysics and given his thought a quite new direction.

CHAPTER SIX

Kant's Reformed Metaphysics

We have now identified the skeptical problems concerning metaphysics to which Kant in his letter to Garve and in the *Prolegomena* attributes his escape from dogmatic slumber in the discipline, and we have seen when and how they roused him. Let us next consider Kant's attempt in the critical philosophy to generate a reformed metaphysics which could be defended against those problems, and his attempt there so to defend it.

I shall begin by trying to say what the reformed metaphysics of the critical philosophy is like (this turns out to be a more difficult task than one might have expected), and how in general terms it has been reformed in order to enable it to cope with the skeptical problems in question.

A first and fundamental point to realize is that Kant is here concerned with metaphysics *as a science*. As he puts it in the *Prolegomena*, "Metaphysics must be a science [*Wissenschaft*] . . . ; otherwise it is nothing at all."[1] We may therefore confine our attention to metaphysics in this strict sense.

This excludes various other sorts of "metaphysics" which Kant mentions from time to time but which do not in his view have a scientific status. In particular, it excludes metaphysics as a mere "natural disposition."[2] And for the *Critique*, though more ambiguously, it evidently also excludes the "metaphysics of morals."[3] (I shall return to the "metaphysics of morals" and its ambiguous status in chapter 10.)

Kant's reflections on skepticism as charted so far suggest that he will be likely to impose the following two requirements on any acceptable science of metaphysics: (1) It should exclude traditional metaphysics' claims about supersensible items, since these run into Pyrrhonian equipollence problems, and instead include all and only those a priori concepts and synthetic a priori principles pertaining by virtue of their general subject matter to the discipline of metaphysics (rather than to mathematics) which seem to be *obviously* legitimate in light of their perspicuity, their confirmation by experience, and their fundamentalness to common sense and natural science (e.g., the concept of cause and the causal principle). (2) It should advance these concepts and principles in such a way that they can be more fully defended against both the Pyrrhonian and the Hume-influenced skeptical problems than by that appearance of obvious legitimacy alone. These, I suggest, were indeed the main requirements which guided Kant in his refashioning of the discipline of metaphysics.

Accordingly, one of Kant's fundamental steps in his reform of metaphysics as a science is to exclude putative information about *supersensible* items, such as the world as a whole, the soul, and God (the subjects of traditional special metaphysics).[4] He recognizes that attaining knowledge of such items has traditionally been the main goal of metaphysics,[5] but he now believes that our knowledge is limited to objects of possible experience in a way that makes this goal unachievable: "We are brought to the conclusion that we can never transcend the limits of possible experience, though that is precisely what this science [of metaphysics] is concerned, above all else, to achieve."[6] Besides the problem of unresolvable equipollence in supersensuous metaphysics, he also has a deeper reason for such pessimism: a fundamental principle which he advances in the *Critique* that all human knowledge requires both concepts and *intuitions*,[7] and that these must indeed include not only pure but *sensible* intuitions,[8] whereas metaphysical claims concerning supersensible items are supported neither by pure nor by sensible intuitions.[9] All that can be done for convictions concerning supersensible items, and even then only in quite limited cases, is to provide a defense of them, not as science or knowledge, but instead merely as morally based faith (*Glaube*),[10] or as non-factual "regulative ideas," i.e., rules whose function is to guide our empirical theorizing in certain fruitful ways.[11]

Accordingly again, in the critical philosophy the core of the science of metaphysics instead comes to consist in what Kant calls "metaphysics of nature" or "immanent physiology"—by which he means a set of very general non-mathematical a priori concepts and synthetic a priori principles governing (both physical and mental) empirical nature.[12] This set includes, and has as its foundation, the concepts and principles treated in the Transcendental Analytic of the *Critique* (or equivalently, the "pure natural science" of *Prolegomena*, part 2).[13] This "metaphysics of nature" includes in a fundamental role such a priori concepts as cause and substance, and such synthetic a priori principles as the causal principle and the principle of the permanence of substance.[14] It bears a strong resemblance, both formally and materially, to traditional general metaphysics, or general ontology, in that, like that traditional discipline, it deals with our most general concepts and principles (at least in a sense), and moreover identifies as such specific concepts and principles which are in many cases the same as those identified as such by that traditional discipline (or at least very similar), for example the concepts of cause and substance and the causal principle.[15]

This "metaphysics of nature" addresses requirement (1), that it should include all and only those a priori concepts and synthetic a priori principles pertaining in virtue of their general subject matter to the discipline of metaphysics which seem *obviously* legitimate in light of their perspicuity, confirmation by experience, and fundamentalness to common sense and natural science. For example, it includes the concept of cause and the causal principle, but it excludes the concept of and principles concerning God.[16]

Moreover, it also addresses requirement (2), that it should advance these a priori concepts and synthetic a priori principles in such a way that they can be more fully defended against the Pyrrhonian and the Hume-influenced skeptical problems than by their appearance of obvious legitimacy alone. It does so in virtue of three special features which more closely define its character, and which should now be described.

First, Kant understands this "metaphysics of nature" to be a priori *but not supersensuous*, a priori *but nonetheless concerned with objects of possible experience*. That might sound self-contradictory at first hearing. However, the notion of a priority which constitutes a distinctive mark of metaphysics for the critical philosophy is *broader* than the notion of supersensuousness which had constituted the distinctive mark of traditional (special) metaphysics.[17] Discriminating between the broader notion of a priority and the narrower notion of supersensuousness indeed constitutes a pivotal move in Kant's project of fashioning a reformed metaphysics that would be defensible against skepticism. (Taking one's cue from the culinary precedent of Hume's "fork"—to which this principle of discrimination is in large part an answer—one might dub this *Kant's sieve*.)

To explain the greater breadth in question, for the significantly different cases of concepts and principles in turn:[18] The supersensuousness of a metaphysical *concept* as conceived by the earlier tradition had consisted simply in the concept's objects or instances not being experienceable—in the everyday sense of "experienceable" in which, for example, tables and their macrophysical properties are "experienceable" but God is not. A concept's a priority, as understood by the critical philosophy, instead consists in the impossibility of deriving the concept without remainder from sensation.[19] Since, the critical Kant believes, we may have concepts which are concepts of objects that are experienced in the everyday sense, yet without these concepts being fully derivable from sensation,[20] it is possible, in his view, for a concept to be a priori without being supersensuous (though not vice versa).[21] The concepts of Kant's "metaphysics of nature," such as the concept of cause, are understood by him to be of precisely this sort—a priori but not supersensuous.[22]

Similarly, concerning *principles*: The supersensuousness of a metaphysical principle as conceived by the earlier metaphysical tradition had consisted in the fact that *the objects and properties to which the principle referred were not experienceable*—again in the

everyday sense of "experienceable" in which, for example, tables and their macro-physical properties are "experienceable"
but God is not. A principle's a priority consists, for the critical
Kant, instead in the subtly different fact that *the principle is not
knowable from experience but only independently thereof* (this time,
unlike in the conceptual case, in the same sense of "experience").[23] Since, the critical Kant believes, there may be principles which we can only know independently of experience but
which nevertheless refer solely to experienceable objects and
properties, it is possible, in his view, for principles to be a priori
without being supersensuous (though, once again, not vice
versa).[24] Kant conceives the principles of his "metaphysics of
nature" to be of just this sort—a priori but not supersensuous.
To give an example which may help to make the distinction
clearer, the causal principle, "Every event has a cause," is understood by Kant to be a principle which refers solely to experienceable objects and properties, namely natural events and
their properties of being caused, but which can nevertheless
only be known independently of experience—the independence of experience deriving, not from a reference to unexperi-
enceable objects and properties, but instead from the *strict universality* asserted by the principle.[25]

Now, the fact that the critical philosophy conceives its "metaphysics of nature" in this whole way—as, though a priori, *not
supersensuous but concerned with objects of possible experience*—enables it to deploy two key strategies for more fully defending
its "metaphysics of nature" against the threat posed by the Pyrrhonian and the Hume-influenced skeptical problems: (a) a
strategy of proving that the concepts and principles of the discipline apply to reality by means of arguments which turn on
showing that application to be a condition of the possibility
of *experience*, i.e., by means of what have come to be known in
the secondary literature as "transcendental arguments";[26] and
(b) a strategy of explaining how we can refer by means of
such concepts and know such principles in terms of their being
cognitive components through which we ourselves constitute
experience, i.e., in terms of what Kant himself calls "transcendental idealism."

A second special feature of Kant's "metaphysics of nature" which helps to make possible a full defense of it against the threat posed by the Pyrrhonian and the Hume-influenced skeptical problems is that it is conceived by Kant to be, not about the world as it is in itself, but instead merely about the world *as (in essential part) constituted by our own minds.*[27] This feature of the "metaphysics of nature" is again essential for enabling it to receive the latter of the two strategies just mentioned for defending its a priori concepts and synthetic a priori principles against the threat posed by such skeptical problems: strategy (b), an explanation of the possibility of such types of cognition in terms of "transcendental idealism."

A third and final special feature of Kant's "metaphysics of nature" which helps to make possible a full defense of it against the threat posed by the Pyrrhonian and the Hume-influenced skeptical problems lies in its *systematicity.*[28] The aspiration to achieve systematicity in metaphysics was not in itself new with Kant; it had already been prominent in Spinoza and Wolff, for example. However, Kant had from an early period rejected their *mathematical* model for generating systematicity in the discipline—specifically, their model of doing so by means of a deductive system of definitions, axioms, and demonstrated theorems—as unsuited to it.[29] And so he needed a new way of achieving systematicity in the discipline. He found this in the system of logical forms of judgment (i.e., roughly, the elemental types of judgment relevant to general logic),[30] and in their (alleged) one-to-one correlation with, first, the fundamental a priori concepts of his new "metaphysics of nature," and thence also its fundamental synthetic a priori principles. As we shall see, this systematicity in Kant's "metaphysics of nature" is essential for the full defense of the discipline against Pyrrhonian equipollence skepticism, as Kant conceives that defense.[31]

This "metaphysics of nature," then, constitutes the core of the critical philosophy's new science of metaphysics. There is also an additional component, though. This is, in effect, a much more richly developed version of the "science of the bounds of human reason" which Kant had already identified as a residual metaphysics in *Dreams of a Spirit Seer.* It includes all of the *Cri-*

tique's various justifications, explanations, and limitations of the sources of a priori knowledge.[32] However, this component has a less secure claim to the title "metaphysics," in Kant's view.[33] So I shall exclude it from consideration as metaphysics for the moment. (I shall return to it, and to the question of its ambiguous status, in chapter 11.)

The above gives, I think, a reasonably full and accurate account of what metaphysics in Kant's central sense of the term, namely, metaphysics *as a science*, does and does not include for the critical philosophy. As I have emphasized, this is a metaphysics remodeled above all in order to enable it to withstand the Pyrrhonian and the Hume-influenced skeptical problems. We should therefore now turn to investigate exactly how its built-in defenses are supposed to work.

CHAPTER SEVEN

Defenses against Humean Skepticism

LET US, THEN, consider Kant's defense of his reformed "metaphysics of nature" against the Pyrrhonian and the Hume-influenced skeptical problems. I shall begin with the Hume-influenced problems, those concerning the existence and reference of a priori concepts and the possibility of synthetic a priori knowledge. For, as we shall see, Kant's solution to the Pyrrhonian problem builds on his solutions to these.

As I have already indicated, Kant's first line of defense here is to point to apparently clear examples of a priori concepts which *do* exist and refer and to apparently clear examples of synthetic a priori principles which *are* known. Some of these examples, including some of the most compelling for Kant, in fact lie outside his reformed "metaphysics of nature" (namely, the concepts and principles of mathematics),[1] but, as we saw, others lie within it (for example, the concept of cause and the causal principle). This is what I have called the *common sense moment* in Kant's solution.

But Kant also develops a much more elaborate solution to the Hume-influenced problems on behalf of his reformed "metaphysics of nature." This solution pursues a dual strategy. One side of the strategy undertakes to *prove that* specific metaphysical a priori concepts refer and specific metaphysical synthetic a priori principles are true. The other side undertakes to *explain the possibility* of their referring and being known.

This dual strategy is reflected in many methodological comments that Kant makes—for example, his famous distinction between an "objective" and a "subjective" side of the Transcendental Deduction.[2] Kant adheres to this dual strategy for defending the concepts and principles of his new "metaphysics of nature" against the Hume-influenced puzzles pretty consistently throughout the Transcendental Analytic of the *Critique*, where the concepts and principles in question are treated.[3] Let us consider each side of this dual strategy in turn.

Kant's *proof that* a specific metaphysical a priori concept refers or a specific metaphysical synthetic a priori principle is true always takes the form of what has come to be known in the secondary literature as a "transcendental argument," i.e., an argument which turns on an attempt to show that the reference or truth in question is *a condition of the possibility of experience* (of a certain type).[4] In other words (since "Y is a condition of the possibility of X" and "Necessarily if X then Y" are logically equivalent), such a proof turns on an attempt to demonstrate the truth of a conditional proposition of the general form "Necessarily if there is experience (of such-and-such a type), then a priori concept C refers / synthetic a priori principle p is true."[5] Most of the work involved in these proofs goes into demonstrating just such a conditional proposition. That done, the completion of the proof—which Kant usually treats as too obvious to require explicit development—is a simple inference by modus ponendo ponens from the truth of this conditional proposition plus the seemingly unquestionable truth of its antecedent ("There is experience [of such-and-such a type]") to the truth of its consequent ("A priori concept C refers / synthetic a priori principle p is true").[6] Examples of such proofs are the Transcendental Deduction (which is concerned with the reference of metaphysical a priori concepts) and the Analogies of Experience (which are concerned with the truth of metaphysical synthetic a priori principles).[7]

One of the main attractions of this style of argument, for Kant, lay in the prospect that it seemed to offer of refuting

Hume-influenced skepticism about metaphysics on behalf of specific metaphysical concepts and principles on the basis of premises which not only Kant but also the Hume-influenced skeptic about metaphysics himself would have to concede, such as that he had experience (of such-and-such a type).[8]

Kant's *explanations of the possibility* of particular metaphysical a priori concepts existing and referring, and of particular metaphysical synthetic a priori principles constituting knowledge, are mainly in terms of his *transcendental idealism*. Famously, the thesis of transcendental idealism holds that the essential form of the objective world which we experience is contributed by our own minds (in contrast to its matter, which is given to us in sensation), this essential form comprising, on the one hand, the pure intuitions of space and time and the synthetic a priori principles of mathematics associated with them, and on the other hand, *the a priori concepts of the understanding and the metaphysical synthetic a priori principles associated with them*.[9] Kant's explanation of the possibility of metaphysical a priori concepts existing and referring is as follows. That they can *exist* at all actually has, in his view, a fairly straightforward explanation (one not strictly dependent on transcendental idealism): instead of being derived passively from sensation, they have their source *in the active understanding*, more specifically, in its logical forms of judgment.[10] For example, the ultimate origin of the concept of cause, and in particular its component concept of necessity, lies in the hypothetical form of judgment "If p then q," which expresses a robust relationship of consequence (*Konsequenz*).[11] That such concepts are able, moreover, to *refer* to objects is explained mainly by the transcendental idealist thesis that they contribute essential form to objects (qua objects of possible experience, or appearances, of course, not things in themselves).[12] For it will be recalled that in his letter to Herz Kant had argued that there were actually *two* circumstances in which the reference of a concept to an object was intelligible: either when the object caused the concept through sensation *or when the concept caused the object*, as notionally happens in the case of a divine archetypal intellect. Kant's mature thesis of transcendental idealism makes the reference of metaphysical a priori concepts intelligible in a secularized version of the latter way: they in a sense cause their objects.[13] A further part of the explanation is supplied by the Schematism chapter of the *Critique*:[14] an account of how the basic logical meanings of these concepts which they derive from the logical forms of judgment get supplemented with temporal "schemata" which make their application to objects of experience possible.[15] For example, in the case of the concept of cause, the basic notion of the consequence of one thing on another that is supplied by the logical form of judgment "If p then q" gets supplemented with what is basically the schema of constant conjunction (à la Hume), which renders the concept applicable to objects of experience.[16]

As for metaphysical synthetic a priori knowledge, transcendental idealism enables Kant to explain the possibility of this in roughly the following way: On the one hand, the fact that certain metaphysical synthetic a priori principles express aspects of the essential form of the objective realm of nature accounts for their truth. On the other hand, the idealist fact that *we* are responsible for the presence of those features accounts for our ability to know that they are there without prior investigation, and hence for the *a priority* of the knowledge in question. How can I know a priori (despite the non-analyticity of the claim) that, for example, every event has a cause? Because *I constitute* reality to conform with this principle.[17]

Such, in general terms, are the strategies by means of which Kant hopes to defend the particular a priori concepts and synthetic a priori principles of his reformed "metaphysics of nature" against the Hume-influenced skeptical puzzles concerning the ability of such concepts to exist and refer and the ability of such principles to constitute knowledge.

CHAPTER EIGHT

Defenses against Pyrrhonian Skepticism

WHAT, NEXT, about the Pyrrhonian problem of a balance of opposing arguments in metaphysics? How does the critical philosophy undertake to save its reformed metaphysics from *this* skeptical problem?

The first point which deserves emphasis here is that Kant evidently saw his solution to the Hume-influenced problems as the key to solving this Pyrrhonian problem as well. This can be seen from the following passage in the *Critique*: "The proper problem of pure reason is contained in the question: How are a priori synthetic judgments possible? [I.e., one of the Hume-influenced problems.—M.N.F.] That metaphysics has hitherto remained in so vacillating a state of uncertainty and contradiction [i.e., the Pyrrhonian equipollence problem—M.N.F.], is entirely due to the fact that this problem . . . has never previously been considered. Upon the solution of this problem . . . depends the success . . . of metaphysics."[1] Indeed, I would suggest that for Kant the importance of the Hume-influenced problems ultimately lay at least as much in the fact that their complete solution promised also to make possible a solution to the Pyrrhonian problem as in the intrinsic force that he saw in them.

How does Kant envisage his solution to the Hume-influenced problems enabling him to save metaphysics from the Pyrrhonian problem as well? *Part* of what he has in mind here is that his solution to the Hume-influenced problems makes possible a solution to *the canonical four Antinomies*. Thus shortly after the passage just quoted he goes on to give as an example of the sort of question that has "always met with unavoidable contradictions" the First Antinomy's question "whether the world has a beginning or is from eternity."[2] To this extent, Kant's idea is that the Hume-influenced problems about (a priori concepts and) synthetic a priori knowledge in metaphysics demand transcendental idealism as part of their solution, and that transcendental idealism then serves as the means for resolving the Antinomies as well.

It does so, according to the *Critique*, by showing the apparent conflicts involved in the Antinomies to be illusory.[3] It accomplishes this in roughly the following way.[4] In the case of the "Mathematical" Antinomies, we have (Kant alleges) compelling arguments both for denying the thesis and for denying the antithesis—e.g., in the First Antinomy, both for denying the thesis that the world has a beginning in time and for denying the antithesis that it lacks a beginning in time and hence is eternal.[5] Since these two possibilities appear to be, not only logically exclusive of each other, but also logically exhaustive, this seems to lead to an unresolvable contradiction, for it seems that we can infer from the disproof of each to the truth of the other. However, if, and only if, we embrace transcendental idealism's claim that the whole spatio-temporal world is merely an appearance, not a thing in itself, then we can escape this apparent contradiction. For in that case, and only in that case, the two possibilities are *not* in fact logically exhaustive after all, since, according to Kant, whenever a subject concept is empty (or, more specifically, self-contradictory)[6] opposite predications concerning it are both false. Consequently, if, and only if, the whole spatio-temporal world is merely apparent (as transcendental idealism holds), then the two equally compelling arguments of a "Mathematical" Antinomy do not really contradict each other after all; both thesis and antithesis can be false, as the arguments (allegedly) prove that they are.[7]

In the case of the "Dynamical" Antinomies, we have (Kant alleges) compelling proofs both for the thesis and for the antithesis—e.g., in the Third Antinomy, both for the thesis that there is freedom, or uncaused causation by the will, and for the antithesis that there is no freedom but instead only thoroughgoing causation. This again seems to leave us with a contradiction. However, if, and only if, transcendental idealism's claim that the realm of nature is merely apparent and distinct from the realm of things as they are in themselves is correct, then the thesis and the antithesis can in fact be, not contradictory, but consistent with each other and both true (namely, of different realms). So, once again, if, and only if, transcendental idealism is true, then these Antinomies can be resolved.[8]

So much for resolving the canonical four Antinomies. However, as I suggested earlier, Kant's concern in the *Critique* about the problem of metaphysics' "vacillating . . . state of uncertainty and contradiction" really still extends beyond the canonical four Antinomies (as in the precritical period). And one may therefore reasonably ask whether his idea of solving this problem via his solution to the Hume-influenced problems does not include more than just the above, relatively well-known, strategies for addressing the four Antinomies. I believe that it does, that it also includes a further, and much less well-known, strategy designed to liberate metaphysics from Pyrrhonian equipollence skepticism more broadly.

Shortly after the passage from the *Critique* recently quoted in which he indicates that the problem of metaphysics' "vacillating . . . state of uncertainty and contradiction" can, and can only, be solved via the solution to the Hume-influenced problem concerning synthetic a priori knowledge, Kant returns to the topic of the problem of "unavoidable contradictions" in metaphysics, describing this as a threat of "dogmatic assertions to which other assertions, equally specious, can always be opposed—that is . . . skepticism."[9] And he indicates the following strategy for solving it: "It must be possible for reason to attain to certainty whether we know [*Wissen*] or do not know [*Nicht-Wissen*] the objects of metaphysics, that is, to come to a decision either in regard to the objects of its enquiries or in regard to the capacity or incapacity of reason to pass any judgment upon them, so that we may either with confidence extend our pure reason or set to it sure and determinate limits."[10] This obscure passage implies, I think, a twofold strategy for addressing the Pyrrhonian equipollence skeptic: on the one hand, produce certain knowledge of some bits of metaphysics by establishing both the facts in question ("the objects of its enquiries") and our ability to know them ("the capacity . . . of reason to pass any judgment upon them"); on the other hand, produce certain knowledge that in relation to other metaphysical matters we do not and cannot have knowledge.[11]

The further twofold strategy that Kant has in mind here is, I suggest, more specifically as follows. First, he believes—not unreasonably, given his understanding of Pyrrhonism as a rather restrained form of skepticism—that his solutions to the Hume-influenced problems on behalf of particular metaphysical concepts and principles by proving that these refer / are true and by explaining the possibility of our achieving reference / knowledge with them are such that the Pyrrhonist is bound to accept these solutions as well. Consider, in particular, Kant's transcendental argument *proofs that*. Kant apparently understands the conditional propositions of the form "Necessarily if there is experience (of such-and-such a type), then a priori concept C refers / synthetic a priori principle p is true" which constitute the core of these proofs to be just as irresistible for a Pyrrhonist, once demonstrated to him, as they are for the Hume-influenced skeptic. For Kant believes the *Critique*'s essential contents generally, and, one must therefore infer, such propositions as these and the demonstrations given for them in particular, to be "the measure, and therefore . . . the paradigm, of all apodeictic . . . certainty."[12] Furthermore, the Pyrrhonist, as Kant conceives him, does not in general question experiential judgments.[13] He is therefore also bound to accept the proposition "There is experience (of such-and-such a type)." Finally, there is no question of Kant's Pyrrhonist questioning logical principles, such as modus ponendo ponens.[14] And so he is bound to infer from those two premises the consequents of the conditional propositions involved: propositions of the form "A priori concept C refers / synthetic a priori principle p is true." A similar points applies to Kant's transcendental idealist *explanations of the possibility* of our referring with / knowing particular metaphysical a priori concepts and synthetic a priori principles: since these explanations are among the essential contents of the *Critique*, they too are evidently understood by Kant to possess "apodeictic . . . certainty."[15] In sum, Kant thinks that the Pyrrhonist cannot but accept the proofs and explanations which he has already given vindicating particular metaphysical concepts and principles. These parts of metaphysics at least can therefore be saved from the threat of a Pyrrhonian balance of opposed arguments in Kant's view.

The second side of Kant's further twofold strategy for freeing metaphysics from the Pyrrhonian problem by building on his solutions to the Hume-influenced problems is as follows. Providing, in the manner just described, a defense that is compelling for the Pyrrhonist of some modest number of metaphysical concepts and principles would in itself settle only a small subset of the myriad "civil wars" between metaphysical claims to which the *Critique* attributes skepticism about the discipline of metaphysics.[16] However, Kant envisages a way of proceeding from this modicum of metaphysical peace to the end of *all* disputes in metaphysics, and hence to the complete liberation of the discipline from the bane of the Pyrrhonian problem. His strategy is not to *settle* the remaining disputes, but rather to show that they do not belong within the discipline of *metaphysics*.

How does he propose to achieve that? One essential pillar supporting his case is his fundamental assumption that metaphysics, properly so called, is of its very essence a science (*Wissenschaft*). (Recall his remark that "metaphysics must be a science . . . ; otherwise it is nothing at all."[17]) This implies, at a minimum, that its principles must not only be true but must also constitute knowledge (*Wissen*). Another essential pillar supporting his case is a conviction that his solutions to the Hume-influenced problems, his proofs and explanations for particular metaphysical a priori concepts and synthetic a priori principles, not only establish that these *do* afford knowledge in the domain of metaphysics, but also furnish a basis for demonstrating that other principles which are currently counted by people as belonging within that domain *cannot* constitute knowledge. This is what he has in mind when he writes that the critical philosophy furnishes in connection with metaphysics "a standard . . . to our judgment whereby knowledge [*Wissen*] may be with certainty distinguished from pseudo-knowledge [*Scheinwissen*]."[18] He believes that the demonstration in question in fact shows that *none* of the principles currently counted by people as falling within the domain of metaphysics *except* for those which he has vindicated in the course of solving the Hume-influenced problems can constitute knowledge. If this can indeed be shown, then, given the fundamental requirement that metaphysics must of its very nature be knowledge, all of these other principles may quite properly be expelled from the domain of metaphysics and left to conduct their "civil wars" elsewhere.[19]

How, though, does Kant hope to demonstrate that all principles currently counted by people as belonging within the domain of metaphysics except for those which he has vindicated in the course of solving the Hume-influenced problems can constitute nothing more than pseudo-knowledge? The answer to this question lies in his conviction that (as he puts it in the *Critique*) "metaphysics . . . is the only science which promises . . . *completion*," and that the critical philosophy can achieve a demonstrably "*complete* cognition" of "reason itself and its pure thinking."[20] By this, he means that the critical philosophy can demonstrate the *completeness* of the conceptual sources and fundamental principles of metaphysical knowledge which it vindicates in answer to the Hume-influenced problems, their *exhaustion* of metaphysical knowledge.

But how can it do that? The demonstration turns crucially on the critical philosophy's claim to show that these conceptual sources and fundamental principles of metaphysical knowledge constitute together an *entire system*.[21] For it is a central and recurrent theme in Kant's thought that the way to demonstrate that an aggregate of items of some particular kind is a *complete* collection of items of that kind is to show that they constitute together, not only all items of that kind which one can discover, but also an *entire system*.[22] (Note that the inference here from *entire* system to *complete* collection is not, as it might initially appear, a trivial one.[23])

Accordingly, in an important passage from the *Von Schön Metaphysics* Kant implies that the full solution to the problem of equipollence skepticism afflicting metaphysics lies, not only in validating specific conceptual sources and fundamental principles of metaphysical knowledge by proving that and explaining how they constitute such, but also in establishing that the sphere of the conceptual sources and fundamental principles of metaphysical knowledge is thereby exhausted through showing that they constitute together an entire system.[24]

The critical philosophy's demonstration in answer to equipollence skepticism that its collection of the conceptual sources and fundamental principles of metaphysical knowledge is complete therefore ultimately rests on the notorious systematic, or "architectonic,"[25] aspects of the *Critique*, which aim to exhibit the entire systematicity of those sources and principles.[26]

More specifically, Kant's idea is as follows: Given that the twelve logical forms of judgment constitute an entire system, it can be demonstrated that our collection of metaphysical a priori concepts of the understanding does so as well by showing that they correspond one-to-one with those logical forms of judgment.[27] And given now that our collection of metaphysical a priori concepts of the understanding constitutes an entire system, it can be shown that our collection of metaphysical synthetic a priori principles does so as well by showing that they in turn correspond one-to-one with the metaphysical a priori concepts of the understanding.[28]

To give a particular example of how these correspondences are supposed to work: the hypothetical form of judgment "If p then q" corresponds to the a priori concept of causation, since it yields the idea of the consequence (*Konsequenz*) of one thing upon another that is the core of the concept of causation;[29] and the a priori concept of causation then in turn corresponds to the synthetic a priori principle that every event has a cause (this time for obvious reasons).

Since, in Kant's view, the *Critique*'s demonstration that its collection of the conceptual sources and fundamental principles of metaphysical knowledge is complete possesses, like the rest of the work's essential contents, "apodeictic . . . certainty," it will again, in his view, be such that the Pyrrhonist cannot but accept it once it is laid out for him. Consequently, the Pyrrhonist can be compelled to admit, not only that these sources and principles provide metaphysical knowledge (in the way explained earlier), but also that all of the remaining principles whose battles have hitherto sullied and might continue to sully the name of the discipline in fact belong outside it.

This, then, is Kant's grand strategy in the critical philosophy for defending a reformed metaphysics against the various skeptical problems that had originally arisen to threaten the discipline in the mid-1760s to early 1770s, causing him to reform it in order to enable it to withstand them. Reformed and defended against those skeptical problems in the ways sketched above, metaphysics at last in the critical philosophy emerges "on the secure path of science."[30] Such, at least, is Kant's belief.

II

Critical Assessment

CHAPTER NINE

Some Relatively Easy Problems

I TURN NOW from pure exposition of Kant's project to some critical assessment of it. I shall begin in this chapter with a consideration of two apparent problems which in fact have fairly straightforward and satisfactory solutions, before proceeding in subsequent chapters to further problems which may be more troublesome. It is my hope that this exercise will shed a little further exegetical light on Kant's project, test its strengths and weaknesses, and also suggest some philosophical morals of broader significance.

A first apparent problem is this rather basic one: Why, given its striking differences from the "metaphysics" of the precritical tradition, does Kant even call the new "metaphysics of nature" which constitutes the core of his reformed metaphysics a "metaphysics" at all?

There is an answer to this question. Although Kant's "metaphysics of nature" cannot simply be equated with either the general metaphysics or the special metaphysics of the precritical tradition, it does nonetheless bear certain important resemblances to each of them. First, as I indicated earlier, it bears a strong formal and material resemblance to precritical general metaphysics, or general ontology. That is why Kant in the *Critique* represents it as the successor-discipline to general ontology.[1] Second, the etymologically derived force of the word "metaphysics," namely that of a discipline dealing with matters "beyond nature" (*meta ta physika*),[2] had been cashed out by precritical metaphysics in terms of the *supersensuousness* which it had understood to pertain to the concepts and principles of general metaphysics in certain areas of their application, but above all to those of special metaphysics.[3] As we saw, Kant in the critical philosophy draws a distinction between such *supersensuousness* as a characteristic of concepts and principles and the broader characteristic of *a priority*, and renounces the former as a feature of the concepts and principles of his own "metaphysics of nature," replacing it with the latter. Accordingly, for him, the notion of *a priority* replaces that of *supersensuousness* as the distinctive mark of "metaphysics" answering to the etymological force of the word: the generic idea of what is "beyond nature" now gets reconceived to mean what is "beyond experience," not in the sense of what is supersensuous, but in the sense of what is *a priori*.[4] This, then, constitutes a further reason for Kant's conception of his "metaphysics of nature" as a "metaphysics": somewhat like traditional metaphysics, and especially traditional special metaphysics, it has, if not quite the supersensuousness which they bore as the distinctive mark of their metaphysicality, then at least the closely related though broader feature of a priority, which now takes over in that role.

A second apparent problem is this: Is there not something odd about Kant's very project of defending metaphysics, given that, as we have seen, the contents and even the general conception of the discipline are for him indeterminate and undergo transformation in the course of the defense? Does this not amount to defending a mere *word*?

Part of the answer to this question has in effect just been supplied: while it is true that for Kant the contents and the general conception of the discipline are to a considerable extent indeterminate and subject to transformation during its defense, there do nonetheless remain certain strong resemblances between the "metaphysics" from which he starts out and the "metaphysics" with which he ends up. A further part of the answer, though, lies in the fact that this shift in the contents and the general conception of the discipline as it undergoes development conforms to a *general* model to which Kant subscribes of how sciences do and should develop. According to his general model, (1) such changes in the contents and conception of a discipline during its development are quite normal, and (2) they represent the gradual emergence to explicitness of an "idea" of the discipline which was implicit in, but only imperfectly grasped by, the minds of inquirers at the start.[5] Moreover, while point (2) seems quite dubious, it is really only point (1) that is essential for addressing the problem with which we are here concerned, and point (1) looks extremely plausible in light of more recent work in the history and philosophy of science.[6]

In short, both of the problems just raised in fact seem to have reasonably straightforward and satisfactory solutions.

CHAPTER TEN

A Metaphysics of Morals?

WE SHOULD now turn to some potentially more serious problems. In this chapter I would like to consider Kant's ambiguous position concerning a "metaphysics of morals." It seems to me that he in fact adopts at least two quietly but radically different positions on this subject during the critical period—first a position which turns out to be flatly self-contradictory, then later a position which avoids such crass inconsistency but which may still be vulnerable to other objections. I shall here concentrate mainly on distinguishing these two positions and identifying the self-contradiction in the first one, merely indicating more briefly at the end some potential problems with the second one.

As I mentioned earlier, the *Critique* already envisages a "metaphysics of morals" in addition to the theoretical metaphysics on which we have focused so far.[1] However, the work seems inclined to exclude this "metaphysics of morals" from the status of metaphysics in the strict sense: "The term 'metaphysics,' in its *strict* sense, is commonly reserved for the metaphysics of speculative reason [i.e., for theoretical metaphysics—M.N.F.]."[2]

What is Kant's reason for this exclusion? Beyond a weak appeal to the precedent set by metaphysical tradition (evident in the passage just quoted), and an equally questionable appeal to an alleged disqualifying empirical component in the concepts dealt with by a "metaphysics of morals,"[3] his main reason lies in his principle, already mentioned, that metaphysics in the strict sense must be a science (*Wissenschaft*), and hence at a minimum knowledge (*Wissen*). For in the *Critique* he denies that there is such a thing as moral or morally based knowledge (*Wissen*).[4] Instead, he only allows there to be moral and morally based cognition (*Erkenntnis*),[5] or faith (*Glaube*).[6]

However, this position turns out to be very problematic on closer inspection. What, to begin with, is the force of the distinction to which Kant implicitly appeals here between *Wissen*, on the one hand, and *Erkenntnis* or *Glaube*, on the other? Kant often uses the word *Erkenntnis* as a *synonym* for *Wissen*.[7] But this obviously cannot be the sense of the word involved here. Instead, his underlying conception here seems to be that *Erkenntnis* (in the relevant sense) is a genus of which *Wissen* is one species, and *Glaube* another.[8] In the *Critique* and in his published *Logic* he defines *Wissen* as a holding-to-be-true which is based on "a cognitive ground which is both objectively and subjectively sufficient."[9] He also implies that the objective sufficiency in question is essentially bound up with intersubjective validity: "what I *know* [*weiß*], I hold to be apodeictically certain, i.e., to be universally and objectively necessary (valid for all)."[10] By contrast, he defines *Glaube* as a holding-to-be-true which is "objectively insufficient, but subjectively sufficient."[11] Thus *Wissen* and *Glaube* share the essential feature that they are based on a *subjectively* sufficient cognitive ground, but what distinguishes them from each other is that *Wissen* is, whereas *Glaube* is not, also based on an *objectively* sufficient cognitive ground.

Accordingly, in the *Critique* Kant evidently means to deny that there could be such a thing as moral or morally based *Wissen* for the reason that morality—and consequently, whatever else is based upon it as well, in particular the "postulates"—lacks an objectively sufficient cognitive ground. (At this stage of his career the failure of the supersensuous "postulates" of the "metaphysics of morals" to constitute *Wissen* is therefore a result of their resting on morality, which fails to constitute *Wissen*—not a result of peculiarities in the *specific way* in which they rest on morality.) For in a key passage at *Critique*, A828–9 / B856–7 he implies that morality, and hence whatever else is based upon it as well, in particular the "postulates," fails to be

Wissen because it is at bottom merely a matter of *sentiments*, and therefore lacks an objectively sufficient cognitive ground—his full thought evidently being that this basis in sentiments makes it (1) only questionably based on cognitive grounds at all, (2) lacking in that reference to something beyond itself which is required for objectivity, and (3) lacking in the intersubjective validity that is required for objectivity.[12]

However, this is very problematic indeed. For the theory that morality—and hence whatever else is based upon it as well—is at bottom merely a matter of *sentiments* is a theory which, while Kant had accepted it in such precritical writings as *Dreams of a Spirit Seer*,[13] he officially and famously *rejects* in the critical period (including the *Critique* itself) in favor of a cognitivist theory of morality.[14] According to the official theory of the critical period, morality instead fundamentally consists in a rational criterion for assessing maxims, or intentions, a rational criterion closely modeled on logical law, specifically on the logical law of contradiction (namely, the "categorical imperative").[15] Morality is therefore (1') certainly based on cognitive grounds, (2') if not exactly in the business of referring to objects, then, at least, as much of a factual matter as logical law is, and (3') as intersubjectively valid as logical law is.[16]

In other words, the sharp cognitivist turn taken by Kant's official moral theory in the critical period quite undercuts his case in the *Critique* for saying that morality—and hence whatever else rests upon it as well—fails to constitute *Wissen* and should therefore be excluded from metaphysics "in its strict sense." His precritical, sentimentalist theory of morality had provided grounds for such a position, but his critical, cognitivist theory of morality does not. And his assumption in the *Critique* that the position is still justified rests on little more than a partial and inconsistent inertia in his thinking.[17]

This problem cuts deeper than the previous ones, revealing a surprisingly fundamental flaw in Kant's thought about metaphysics in the *Critique*. Still, in one sense it remains a modest problem. For it points, not to any weakness in Kant's defense of his theoretical metaphysics in the face of skeptical problems, but rather towards a perhaps needlessly missed opportunity to complement that theoretical metaphysics with a metaphysics of morals enjoying equal status with it as *Wissen* and *Wissenschaft*, and possibly even including certain principles concerning the supersensible (the "postulates"). And Kant might on reflection have rather welcomed such an opportunity.

Indeed, I think that he eventually *did* welcome it. The *Groundwork of the Metaphysics of Morals* (1785) for the most part stays faithful to the *Critique*'s position that morality—and hence whatever is based upon it as well—constitutes only *Erkenntnis*, not *Wissen* or *Wissenschaft*.[18] However, the tendency in Kant's subsequent ethical writings is towards *exploiting* the opportunity to promote morality, and what is based upon it, to the status of *Wissen* and *Wissenschaft*. This process already begins in the *Critique of Practical Reason* (1788), where, although the main body of the work conforms to the preceding texts in characterizing morality, and hence whatever is based on it, as merely *Erkenntnis*, rather than *Wissen* or *Wissenschaft*,[19] the very end of the work switches to emphasizing that they have the status of *Wissenschaft*,[20] and then the preface (which was presumably written last) describes morality and the postulate of transcendent freedom based upon it—though not the other two postulates, God and human immortality—as *Wissen*.[21] The *Critique of Judgment* (1790) continues this new position, arguing that the postulate of freedom is knowable (*scibile*),[22] though the other two postulates are not, but merely constitute faith (*Glaube*).[23] Unlike in the *Critique*, the reason for these other two postulates' shortfall from knowability is now not that morality itself falls short of being knowledge, but rather that the specific nature of the link between morality and these postulates is too weak for its status as knowledge to transfer to them; in contrast to transcendent freedom, which is a strict precondition of morality, the *summum bonum* of a correspondence between level of moral virtue and level of happiness, and hence the postulation of the God and human immortality that are required for its realization, is merely something like an aspiration that inevitably accompanies morality.[24] With this whole shift in position, the metaphysics of morals is elevated to virtual parity with the metaphysics of nature: now it too, at least in important part, claims to contain genuine *Wissen* and *Wissenschaft*; indeed, it even claims to provide genuine *Wissen* of one noumenal fact, namely transcendent freedom.[25]

This later position of Kant's is radically different from his earlier one in the *Critique*. It certainly has the virtue of avoiding the crass inconsistency that afflicted the earlier position. But is it defensible? Deciding this would require little less than a full assessment of Kant's moral philosophy, which is well beyond the scope of this essay. But the following are some of the questions on which a verdict would turn: (1) Is Kant's cognitivist account of morality correct (rather than, say, a sentimentalist account like the one to which he had himself once been attracted)? (2) Does morality really presuppose *transcendent* freedom (rather than merely a type of freedom that is compatible with the thoroughgoing causal determination found in nature)? (3) Even if the answer to both of those questions were positive, would not the essential location of the freedom presupposed by morality in the realm of things in themselves, which according to Kant's official account in the *Critique* are unknowable, simply make both it and our moral judgments concerning particular obligations and characters unknowable?[26] (Perhaps we can know that *if* people have transcendent freedom, then they stand under such and such moral obligations and have such and such moral characters, but not that either of these things is actually so.) (4) Is Kant's picture of a somewhat weaker link between moral obligation and the *summum bonum*, and hence the postulates of God and human immortality, correct? Is it not rather the case that there is simply no intimate (i.e., more than just locally psychological) link here at all?

CHAPTER ELEVEN

Failures of Self-Reflection

KANT'S PROJECT also seems to face some more fundamental problems, however. As I mentioned earlier, in addition to his "metaphysics of nature," he also recognizes a further component of his new science of metaphysics, namely a more fully developed version of the "science of the bounds of human reason" which he had first identified as metaphysics in *Dreams of a Spirit Seer*, and which in its mature form includes all of the *Critique*'s various justifications, explanations, and limitations of the sources of a priori knowledge. As I also noted, though, he only allows this further component of his new metaphysics a less secure claim to the title of "metaphysics." I want to suggest that this ambiguity of status serves to paper over some deep problems which afflict the parts of his position in question, and which thereby infect the rest of his position as well, in particular the "metaphysics of nature" itself.

The problems in question all share a somewhat similar general character. In each case they consist in what might be called a *failure of self-reflection* on Kant's part (ironically, of course, given the highly self-reflective aspirations and reputation of his work). By this I mean, roughly, a failure to take sufficient account of a danger that in the course of addressing philosophical difficulties facing claims of a certain sort by making some further claims, one's further claims may themselves be running into philosophical difficulties similar to those faced by the original claims, and perhaps even in a more severe form.

(Such failures of self-reflection are surprisingly common in the history of philosophy. Examples would be the weakness which Plato eventually identified in his own theory of forms in the *Parmenides'* Third Man Argument, and the weakness afflicting logical positivism's thesis that all meaningful propositions are either tautologies or empirically verifiable that this thesis itself seems to fit into neither of those two allegedly exhaustive categories.)

Let us consider, first, a problem which threatens Kant's strategy of using transcendental arguments in order to prove that particular metaphysical synthetic a priori principles are true. The problem concerns the status of the conditional propositions that lie at the heart of such proofs: "Necessarily if there is experience (of such-and-such a type), then synthetic a priori principle p is true." What is the status of these conditional propositions supposed to be? It is clear that, for Kant, they must be a priori.[1] What is much less clear is whether he regards them as *analytic* a priori or instead as *synthetic* a priori (both interpretations have found champions in the secondary literature).[2] Now, it seems to me that this ambiguity papers over a serious problem. The problem can be put in the form of the following dilemma: Clearly, these key conditional propositions must be either analytic or synthetic (since the "syntheticity" of a proposition is in effect simply defined as its non-analyticity). Suppose, first, that they were analytic. It seems that in order for that to be so, their justifications—which, as I noted earlier, in fact make up the bulk of transcendental arguments—would have to take the form of successive stages of analyzing the concept of "experience (of such-and-such a type)," or "objects of experience (of such-and-such a type)," until the analysis yielded the thought of the application of the putatively synthetic a priori principle p in question to the relevant (objects of) experience. But now, it also seems that if such an undertaking were successful, then it would show that the consequents of the conditional propositions in question—in our schema, the principles p—were after all *analytic* rather than synthetic. For, as this strategy of justification implies, and as Kant indeed himself never tires of saying explicitly,[3] *these principles p must in the end be interpreted as re-*

stricted in their scope to relevant (objects of) experience. Consequently, if analysis of the very concept of the relevant (objects of) experience yielded the thought asserted in these principles p, then these principles p would also themselves be implicitly analytic.[4] To use the Second Analogy as an example: On this interpretation, it would turn out that the proposition "Necessarily if there is experience of objective temporal events, then the principle that everything has a cause is true" was established by analyzing the concept of experience of objective temporal events until the thought of the universality of causation was found lying implicitly within that concept. But this would only show that everything *that is an experienceable objective temporal event* has a cause, and indeed Kant explicitly insists that we must interpret the principle that everything has a cause in this restricted way.[5] But now, once this force of the principle is made explicit, is it not clear that, if the analysis had indeed shown what it purported to have shown, then it would also have shown that the principle that everything has a cause was itself implicitly analytic? In short, undertaking to show that *synthetic* a priori principles were true by using transcendental arguments which turned on conditional propositions which were analytic would be self-defeating. That is one horn of the dilemma. Let us, then, try the alternative interpretation, namely that the conditional propositions in question are instead *synthetic* a priori. In that case, they will obviously have to be *metaphysical* synthetic a priori propositions (not mathematical ones), in virtue of their subject matter. Therefore, they, just as much as the metaphysical synthetic a priori principles p which it is Kant's ultimate concern in these transcendental arguments to demonstrate, will stand in need of a justification before they may be accepted. For Kant requires—and reasonably so, in the light of the vacillating state of metaphysical belief and the plausibility of Hume's fork—that no synthetic a priori proposition of metaphysics be accepted until it has received a satisfactory justification.[6] Accordingly, as has already been mentioned, attempts to justify these conditional propositions do in fact form the bulk of Kant's transcendental arguments. Under the interpretation which we are considering, such a justification will evidently have to proceed from the idea of the relevant type of (objects of) experience to the application of the synthetic a priori principle p ultimately undergoing proof by means of steps which, while some of them may be analytic, will include at least one that is synthetic (otherwise, the conditional proposition would not be synthetic, as the interpretation we are considering says, but analytic). Moreover, this synthetic step will have to be synthetic *a priori*, not synthetic *a posteriori* (otherwise, the conditional proposition would itself be a posteriori, contrary to Kant's conception of it as a priori). In other words, there will have to be at least one *synthetic a priori* step in the justification establishing the key conditional proposition. However, this creates a problem. For (once again) this step will obviously have to be a *metaphysical* synthetic a priori proposition (not a mathematical one), in virtue of its subject matter, and so it, just as much as the conditional proposition which it is being adduced to support, and the principle p which it is Kant's ultimate concern to demonstrate, will stand in need of a justification before it may be accepted. But this seems to launch us on an infinite regress. For, whichever general form the justification is going to take—whether that already being applied to principle p itself or that already being applied to the conditional proposition adduced in support of principle p (these seem to exhaust the possibilities available to Kant)—it will have to invoke at least one new metaphysical synthetic a priori proposition. But this will again stand in need of a justification before it may be accepted. And so on ad infinitum.[7] In short, any attempt to demonstrate the synthetic a priori principles of Kant's metaphysics by means of transcendental arguments whose key conditional propositions were themselves *synthetic* a priori would turn out—once again—to be self-defeating. This is the second horn of the dilemma. In sum, it seems that Kant's very enterprise of demonstrating metaphysical synthetic a priori principles by means of transcendental arguments is implicitly incoherent.[8]

An analogous dilemma confronts those transcendental arguments which aim to prove *the reference of a priori concepts*. Here again, the crucial conditional propositions involved—"Necessarily if there is experience (of such-and-such a type), then a priori concept C refers"—must obviously be a priori, and therefore either synthetic a priori or analytic a priori. If they are synthetic a priori, then we run into the same infinite regress problem we just encountered as the second horn of the previous dilemma. If, on the other hand, they are analytic a priori, then they will presumably have to be established by showing the concept of the relevant type of (objects of) experience to contain, upon conceptual analysis, the a priori concepts whose reference is to be proved. But this would entail that the concept of the relevant type of (objects of) experience *was itself implicitly a priori*. And in that case the Hume-influenced skeptic concerning a priori concepts who is supposed to be addressed by these arguments and who is assumed in them to be conceding that we have the relevant type of (objects of) experience would in fact have had no business making any such concession in the first place.

A failure of self-reflection also afflicts Kant's transcendental idealist *explanations of the possibility* of referring by means of a priori concepts and having knowledge of synthetic a priori propositions. Prima facie at least, these explanations seem to confront the following two problems. (1) Kant's considered view must be that these explanations are not only in some sense metaphysical, but also synthetic a priori—for he does not suppose them to be either analytic or known from experience,[9] and could not plausibly do so. Now Kant demands an explanation of how synthetic a priori knowledge is possible in general, and moreover lays it down as a principle—a reasonable one, in light of the vacillating state of metaphysical belief and the plausibility of Hume's fork—that no synthetic a priori proposition in metaphysics should be accepted until the question of how it can be known has been satisfactorily solved.[10] However, this seems to lead to the following difficulty: The only such explanation that Kant has (either for mathematics or for metaphysics) is in terms of transcendental idealism's thesis of mind-imposition. But clearly, he does not think that the synthetic a priori thesis of transcendental idealism is *itself* known in virtue of its being mind-imposed. Nor, on the face of it, would an attempt to explain it in that way even be coherent—for that would amount to saying that we can know the synthetic a priori thesis that the mind imposes such and such principles on things in themselves because this thesis is itself imposed by the mind on things in themselves. So it seems that concerning the central thesis of transcendental idealism itself we are left without any answer to Kant's fundamental question of how synthetic a priori knowledge is possible; and moreover, that, since this is a metaphysical thesis, by Kant's own principles we must therefore refrain from asserting it. (2) It seems that the thesis of transcendental idealism is understood by Kant, and indeed must be understood by him, as a thesis about things in themselves—specifically, as a thesis about the mind *in itself* imposing principles on things *in themselves*. But then any claim to *know* this thesis conflicts with Kant's central doctrine—grounded in his principle that our knowledge requires both concepts and intuitions, and that the nature of our concepts and intuitions limits us to a knowledge of mere appearances; together with his theory that in order even to achieve *reference*, our most fundamental concepts, the a priori concepts of the understanding, need to be schematized in temporal terms, and thereby rendered applicable to objects of possible experience, but also *in*applicable to atemporal things in themselves—that we cannot know anything at all about things in themselves.[11] These, then, are the two problems that Kant's *explanations of possibility* appear to face.[12]

Kant seems not to have noticed these problems at all in the first edition of the *Critique*. There he writes with blithe self-confidence as though no such problems were even on the horizon: "I have to deal with nothing save reason itself and its pure thinking; and to obtain complete cognition of these, there is no need to go far afield, since I come upon them in my own self."[13]

By the time of writing the preface to the second edition he seems to have become more aware of the problems. Thus, evincing at least some awareness of problem (1), he now discusses the question of the character and basis of the thesis of transcendental idealism at considerable length.[14] And evincing some awareness of problem (2), he now notes in connection with this thesis that "the propositions of pure reason, especially if they venture out beyond all limits of possible experience, cannot be brought to the test through any experiment with their *objects*, as in natural science."[15]

What is his response to these problems? Essentially, he seems to argue as follows: If invoked directly to explain metaphysical knowledge, the thesis of transcendental idealism could have no more than the status of a hypothesis,[16] which would be unsatisfactory,[17] in particular because, as referring to things in themselves, it would be a hypothesis that could in principle neither be confirmed nor refuted by investigation of its objects.[18] However, the thesis does admit of being "proved, apodeictically not hypothetically, from the nature of our representations of space and time and from the elementary concepts of the understanding."[19] That is to say, it admits of conclusive proof by being shown to be the only satisfactory explanation of our possession of synthetic a priori knowledge concerning space and time in mathematics, and of our referring by means of the a priori concepts of the understanding.[20] In addition, according to Kant, the thesis is further proved by its being the only satisfactory solution to the contradictions of the Antinomies.[21]

However, this all remains quite problematic. To the extent that problem (1) is supposed to be answered by this account, the answer seems unsatisfactory in at least the following two respects. First, Kant has here in effect offered us a *proof that*—or rather, several proofs that—the metaphysical synthetic a priori thesis of transcendental idealism is true: the only way we could have synthetic a priori knowledge in mathematics, refer by means of the a priori concepts of the understanding, etc., is if this thesis were true; we do have such knowledge, achieve such reference, etc.; therefore the thesis is true. However, he has still offered us no *explanation how* it can be known, such as the thesis itself furnishes for other synthetic a priori knowledge. Clearly, though, it was his original position that merely providing proofs without complementary explanations would be an insufficient answer to puzzlement about synthetic a priori knowledge, and insufficient justification for advancing synthetic a priori claims in metaphysics. That is one difficulty. A second is the following. Someone might, perhaps, respond to such a criticism, on Kant's behalf, that the revised, lowered standard which he is now in effect accepting for at least some metaphysical synthetic a priori claims—namely, a standard of merely providing proofs without complementary explanations—is in fact a reasonable one. However, such a defense would not save the thesis of transcendental idealism from its troubles—rather the contrary. For one thing, requiring an explanation as well as a proof in each case still seems a reasonable demand, given the puzzling nature of synthetic a priori knowledge. For another thing, such a defense would prompt the very awkward question, Why, then, should not normal mathematical proofs that the synthetic a priori principles of mathematics are true and Kant's transcendental argument proofs that the a priori concepts of the understanding refer likewise be sufficient for *these* cases? In other words, what need of recourse in addition to the thesis of transcendental idealism in order to explain such cognition? In short, the main argument for believing in transcendental idealism in the first place would have been undercut.[22] Moreover, the situation still seems at least as bad in relation to problem (2). For the preface of the second edition, whatever its further details, still seems committed to transcendental idealism being *a thesis about things in themselves which is nevertheless known*. And that still produces a conflict with Kant's official position that things in themselves are unknowable. In sum, while the preface of the second edition does at least get as far as noticing and responding to problems (1) and (2) to a certain extent, its responses seem unsatisfactory. Nor is it easy to see how these problems *could* be solved within a recognizably Kantian framework.

A final arguable failure of self-reflection concerns the architectonic part of Kant's answer to skepticism about metaphysics—his attempt to demonstrate the *entire systematicity* (and thence completeness) of the collections of a priori concepts and synthetic a priori principles which comprise his new "metaphysics of nature." As I noted earlier, his approach here is, essentially, to demonstrate the entire systematicity of the synthetic a priori principles which he has included in the discipline by matching them one-to-one with the a priori concepts of the discipline, presupposing that the latter themselves form an entire system; and to demonstrate the entire systematicity of these a priori concepts in turn by matching them one-to-one with the logical forms of judgment (i.e., roughly, the elemental forms of judgment relevant for general logic), presupposing that the latter form an entire system. However, this is obviously a series of promissory notes that cannot be continued indefinitely. And accordingly, this series of referrals does in fact come to an end once we reach the logical forms of judgment. The question then arises, though, How can Kant know that his collection of the logical forms of judgment constitutes an entire system?

Now one certainly cannot accuse Kant of overlooking this question *altogether*, because he does suggest answers to it. However, his answers do not in the end seem satisfactory, and do arguably at least bespeak insufficient attention to the question.

His case for the entire systematicity (and hence completeness) of his collection of logical forms of judgment is evidently that, once properly arranged, they can in some sense be *seen* to form an entire system (though, no doubt, only by a theoretically tutored eye). This is the point of the following systematic-looking arrangement of them in the *Critique*, which Kant prefaces with the revealing comment that it "shows [*vor Augen stellen*]" that an exhaustive statement of the forms of judgment can easily be given.[23]

I
Quantity of Judgments

Universal
Particular
Singular

II *Quality*		III *Relation*
Affirmative		Categorical
Negative		Hypothetical
Infinite		Disjunctive

IV
Modality

Problematic
Assertoric
Apodeictic

Now suppose that we were to grant, for the sake of argument, that the arrangement of the forms of judgment in this table is a reasonable one, and does show their systematicity (a rather generous concession, of course). Even so, the idea that the table shows them to constitute an *entire* system would still require further support. In particular, we would still need a reason for believing that the table exhausts its system *horizontally* (that there are no further groups besides the four listed in the table) and a reason for believing that it does so *vertically* (that there are in each group no more than the three forms listed by the table). How does Kant propose to show these things?

Consider *horizontal* exhaustiveness first. As Reinhard Brandt has convincingly argued, the principle that governs the inclusion of all and only the four groups " I Quantity," "II Quality," "III Relation," and "IV Modality" is the traditional division of logic into a treatment of 1. concepts, 2. judgments, 3. syllogisms, and 4. a doctrine of method. "I Quantity" concerns the (subject-)concepts used in judgments; "II Quality" the affirmation or denial constitutive of judgment as such; "III Relation" the three types of major premises which distinguish the three traditional forms of syllogism;[24] and "IV Modality" the connection between judgment and the mind that employs it in order to arrive at knowledge.[25] Kant's deeper picture seems to be roughly that the raison d'être of *concepts* is to function in *judgments*,[26] while that of judgments is to function in *syllogisms*, and thereby to lead to *knowledge*—so that one should expect all of these aspects to be somehow inscribed in the very form of a judgment.[27]

Concerning *vertical* exhaustiveness, Kant develops quite an imaginative solution.[28] His idea here seems to be that within each group of three forms of judgment one can see that the three exhaust the group because they are such that the first and the second are in a way opposites, while the third is in a way their synthesis,[29] though not in a way that would render it simply analyzable into them (since that would be incompatible with its status as an *elemental*, or primitive, form of judgment).[30] He does not explicitly develop this idea in application to each group, but it is not too difficult to see the sort of thing that he has in mind. Consider, first, the *quantitative* forms of judgment: The *universal* form of judgment ("All As . . .") and the *particular* form ("Some As . . .") are in a way opposite to each other, while the *singular* form ("This A . . .") in a way combines the former's focus on a totality (now a singular totality) with the latter's specification of a subset (now a singular subset), though in a way that does not make it simply analyzable in terms of them.[31] Consider, next, the *qualitative* forms of judgment: The *affirmative* form of judgment comprises purely positive judgments, such as "Men are mortal," the *negative* form of judgment judgments which involve propositional negation, such as "It is not the case that men are mortal," and the *infinite* form of judgment (despite its misleading name) judgments which involve predicate-negation, such as "Men are not-mortal." Now it is easy enough to see that one might with some plausibility characterize the first two of these forms as opposites and the third as a sort of synthesis of them,[32] though a synthesis that does not make it simply analyzable in terms of them.[33] Consider, next, the *relational* forms of judgment: The *categorical* form of judgment simply affirms a proposition, the *hypothetical* form ("If p then q") affirms neither of its two contained propositions, and is in that sense the opposite of the former, while the *disjunctive* form ("p or q [or r . . .]") in a way combines the categorical form's affirmation with the hypothetical form's non-affirmation, in that it affirms that one of its contained propositions is true but without specifying which one,[34] though in a way which does not involve its analyzability into the other two forms.[35] Finally, consider the *modal* forms of judgment: The *problematic* form expresses mere possibility, whereas the *assertoric* form expresses reality, which is in a sense the opposite of mere possibility, while the *apodeictic* form expresses necessity,[36] or in other words reality in all possible cases,[37] and thereby in a way combines the former two, though in a way that does not make it simply analyzable in terms of them.[38] So Kant does have quite an imaginative strategy for solving the problem of *vertical* exhaustiveness which is at least somewhat plausible.[39]

Kant's attempt to show that he has an entire system (and hence a complete collection) of the elemental forms of judgment relevant to general logic is thus rather ingenious. Nonetheless, there are grounds for skepticism, including the following. (1) Concerning horizontal exhaustiveness, Kant himself perceives a break between the logical-content-oriented rationales behind the first three groups and the epistemological rationale behind the fourth;[40] and modern logicians would exclude the traditional doctrine of method, with its epistemological focus, from logic.[41] Nor is it easy to see why further groups might not be *added*—for example, a new group "Rule" (after all, Kant himself characterizes the understanding as a faculty of rules,[42] and very plausibly sees rules as fundamental to concepts,[43] judgments,[44] and syllogisms[45] alike). (2) Concerning vertical exhaustiveness, the criterion of opposition-and-synthesis-but-without-analyzability which Kant invokes here needs to be interpreted so flexibly in order to accommodate the forms of judgment involved that one wonders whether it really constitutes much of a constraint at all (could not almost any three forms of judgment be made to fit this model, and in almost any order?). Also, even if it does, what precludes the possibility that the pattern might be reiterated at further levels (as Fichte and Hegel later envisaged)? (3) In order for a display such as Kant provides in his table of logical forms of judgment to constitute a plausible demonstration of entire systematicity, and hence complete collection, it would at least have to include all *known* elemental forms of judgment relevant to general logic. However, this table seems not to. Indeed, it does not even seem to include all those known *to Kant*. Consider, for example, group "III Relation." Even if one accepts as reasonable Kant's general rationale for this group, namely providing the elemental forms of judgment required to serve as major premises in valid forms of syllogism (i.e., *mediated* inference), what about "p *vel* q," a form of judgment which serves as a major premise in the valid syllogisms "p *vel* q, -p therefore q" and "p *vel* q, -q therefore p"? This form of judgment is not equivalent or reducible to Kant's categorical, hypothetical, or disjunctive forms (since *his* disjunctive form involves not *vel* but instead the exclusive *aut*, and his hypothetical form involves not mere material implication, which would arguably make a reduction possible,[46] but instead a more robust notion of consequence [*Konsequenz*], which obstructs a reduction). And yet this form of judgment and its function in syllogisms must have been familiar to Kant, especially given his good knowledge of Latin. Moreover, if the rationale for this group were broadened to include elemental forms of judgment which serve as premises in valid forms of inference more generally (not only valid syllogistic, or mediated, forms of inference), as seems entirely reasonable, then should not the conjunctive form "p & q" be included here? This form supports the immediate inferences "p & q therefore p" and "p & q therefore q"; it is not equivalent or reducible to Kant's categorical, hypothetical, or disjunctive forms; and it was of course well known to Kant.[47] (4) Notoriously, Kant believed that general logic was "a closed and completed body of doctrine" that had in all essentials already been completed by Aristotle.[48] The dramatic falsification of this belief that occurred with Frege's development of quantificational logic in the nineteenth century has made the inadequacy of Kant's table of forms of judgment even more apparent, adding, as it does, many further types of inference not accounted for by Kant's table.[49]

In the end, therefore, Kant's attempt to demonstrate the entire systematicity of his collection of logical forms of judgment seems inadequate, and their entire systematicity consequently unproven. Moreover, since it is his claim of their entire systematicity that underpins his claims that his collections of metaphysical a priori concepts and metaphysical synthetic a priori propositions constitute entire systems, this situation entails that the latter claims are unproven as well.

Such, then, are the failures of self-reflection which appear to undermine the "science of the bounds of human reason" component of Kant's new metaphysics, and thereby also his new "metaphysics of nature" itself.

CHAPTER TWELVE

The Pyrrhonist's Revenge

A FINAL, and perhaps the most fundamental, problem for Kant's project which should be discussed might be dubbed *the Pyrrhonist's revenge.*

As I have emphasized, Kant interprets Pyrrhonism as modest in the scope of its skeptical attack, in particular as normally exempting empirical, mathematical, moral, and logical claims—and instead focusing its attack just on the claims of metaphysics.

Kant's strategy for addressing Pyrrhonism presupposes this interpretation of it as a moderate form of skepticism. In particular, Kant's strategy presupposes that Pyrrhonists do not challenge the assumptions that one has experience of certain types or that classical logical principles are valid, so that in answering their attack on metaphysics Kant can draw on such assumptions in order to frame transcendental arguments in support of the claims which they *do* challenge—specifically, on the assumptions that "There is experience (of such-and-such a type)," or "I have experience (of such-and-such a type)," and that modus ponendo ponens is a valid form of logical argument.

Indeed, this presupposition of the moderation of Pyrrhonism underpins Kant's project of defending metaphysics against skepticism in broader ways as well. For one thing, his use of transcendental arguments against both the Hume-influenced and the Pyrrhonian skeptic is not only ad hominem, but also *endorses* the arguments, and in particular their key assumptions

that there is experience of certain types and that modus ponendo ponens is valid. That Kant feels able to make such assumptions himself is due to his conviction that they are not
vulnerable to skeptical attack (in particular, not from the quarter of Pyrrhonian skepticism).

For another thing, as we have seen, Kant frames the central
epistemological question of the critical philosophy as the question "How is synthetic a priori knowledge possible?" But in
doing so, he implies that the problematic character of this type
of knowledge contrasts with the *unproblematic* character of two
other types of knowledge, namely synthetic *a posteriori* knowledge and *analytic* a priori knowledge—in other words, knowledge based on *experience* and on *logic* (or more specifically, the
logical law of contradiction), respectively. So here again he implies that the claims of experience and logic are not vulnerable
to skeptical attack (in particular, not from the quarter of Pyrrhonian skepticism).

Now Kant's interpretation of Pyrrhonism as a moderate sort
of skepticism is in fact very questionable. Shortly after Kant
developed his position, Hegel argued forcefully in his 1802
essay *The Relation of Skepticism to Philosophy* and again later in
his *Lectures on the History of Philosophy*, against interpretations
like Kant's,[1] that Pyrrhonism was actually a far more radical
form of skepticism, a form of skepticism that attacked (virtually)
all beliefs.[2] And while Kant's line of interpretation is not without its defenders today (most prominent among them, Michael
Frede), it is probably fair to say that, in one form or another,
the alternative line of interpretation proposed by Hegel is today
the preferred one—so that, for example, the contemporary authority on Pyrrhonism Myles Burnyeat reads Pyrrhonism in
more or less the same way as Hegel did.[3]

In itself, this situation is not particularly threatening to
Kant's philosophical position. For one thing, Kant in fact acknowledges that there were *certain strands* of Pyrrhonism (and
also Academic skepticism) which took the more extreme form
of calling all beliefs into question—though he distinguishes
these from the orthodox Pyrrhonism of Pyrrho himself, and
considers them inferior to it, because excessive and self-

defeating.[4] For another thing, and more importantly, what really matters for Kant's philosophical project is, not that he have read the history of philosophy correctly, but that he have taken into account whatever version or variant of Pyrrhonism has *real philosophical force*, and even if his reading of Pyrrhonism were mistaken, his intuition that any form of Pyrrhonism which attacked all beliefs, in particular beliefs in experience and in the principles of classical logic, would be excessive and self-defeating might still be right, and if so would warrant his philosophical stance.

But *is* it right? Kant's judgment that unrestricted forms of Pyrrhonian skepticism are *self-defeating* actually seems mistaken, or at best naive. He argues, in this vein, that such extreme skeptics "contradicted themselves, for they said that everything is uncertain without distinction and nonetheless they maintained their propositions and attributed to them infallible certainty."[5] However, versions of this sort of complaint had already been raised against the Pyrrhonists in antiquity,[6] and had already been cleverly taken into account and forestalled by such unrestricted ancient Pyrrhonists as Sextus Empiricus. Their solution was that, while their skeptical doubt did indeed apply unrestrictedly to all *beliefs* or *assertions of fact*, including even their own positions if adopted as such, they would retain allegiance to their own positions not in that way but instead merely as expressions of how matters *appeared* to them to be.[7]

Much less clearly misguided, though, is Kant's further objection that in attempting to attack such judgments as those of experience and logic an unrestricted skepticism is *excessive*—in the sense that no plausible skeptical attack is really possible in such areas. This is therefore the objection on which I would like to focus here.

This normative assessment too actually turns out to be highly questionable in the end. One philosopher who recognized this early and clearly was again Hegel, who argued for the viability of Pyrrhonian attacks even against judgments of subjective— and a fortiori against judgments of objective—experience,[8] and against logical judgments.

Hegel encountered Kant's normative assessment, not so much in Kant's own formulation of it, but rather in the reformulation that it had received at the hands of the neo-Kantian self-styled "skeptic" G. E. Schulze. Keeping this in mind, let us consider the question of subjective experience first and then that of logic second.

In his book *Aenesidemus* of 1792 Schulze had argued explicitly that no skeptic attacks judgments of subjective experience.[9] In his 1802 essay *The Relation of Skepticism to Philosophy*, Hegel forcefully criticizes Schulze's assumption that judgments of subjective experience are certain and beyond skeptical attack. He argues that, on the contrary, any Pyrrhonism worth its salt will apply its equipollence method not only against judgments of other sorts but also against those of subjective experience.[10] (He is even more scathingly critical of Schulze's additional position that some judgments of *objective* experience are certain and beyond serious skeptical doubt. As he rightly notes, creating plausible doubts about such judgments was the very stock-in-trade of ancient Pyrrhonism.[11])

Hegel does not elaborate on this point about subjective experience in order to show exactly *how* a Pyrrhonian skeptical attack on it did or might go. However, one can fill in his omission easily enough. For example, near the start of *Against the Logicians* Sextus Empiricus adduces against those people who have convictions in their own appearances the counterargument that "some of the physicists, like Democritus, have abolished all appearances."[12] Famously, Democritus had argued that all that existed were atoms and the void, and Sextus's thought here is evidently that this implies the unreality of even subjective appearances.[13] Sextus does not usually pursue this sort of attack to its bitter end—instead tending to spare subjective experience from attack.[14] However, the historical evidence shows that other ancient Pyrrhonists did so.[15] In our own day a Pyrrhonist might plausibly draw for this purpose on the cleverly argued positions (strikingly similar to Democritus's) of such eliminative materialists as Paul Feyerabend, Richard Rorty, and the Churchlands. By generating a counterargument against self-ascriptions of subjective experience in this way, he can, it seems, very well hope to call even such judgments into question.

It may be thought that Pyrrhonism faces serious obstacles here, though. In particular, Sextus himself and later, more famously, Descartes suggest that there is a good reason why subjective experience must be exempted from skeptical attack, namely because a person's current subjective experience *necessitates* his acknowledgment (or belief or knowledge) of it, so that he *cannot* question it.[16]

This argument does not in the end seem compelling, however, for several reasons. First, the principle that one's current possession of subjective experience necessitates acknowledgment (or belief or knowledge) of it looks like just the sort of dogmatic principle that the Pyrrhonian skeptic is adept at calling into question through counterargument. An especially attractive resource for a counterargument to draw on in this case would be the phenomenon of *unconscious* subjective experiences. Second, the inference from that principle as a premise to the intermediate conclusion that the skeptic must acknowledge (or believe or know) that he currently has subjective experience would require the further premise that *he currently has subjective experience*. But, of course, in relation to a skeptic who is proposing to call his own current subjective experience into question such a premise would be flagrantly question-begging. Third (and perhaps less obviously), the inference from the intermediate conclusion that the skeptic must acknowledge (or believe or know) that he has his current subjective experience to the further conclusion that he cannot skeptically question it is dubious. For, counterintuitive though this may sound at first hearing, people quite often find themselves in a condition which would naturally be described as one of both believing that p and suspending belief on the question whether or not p. Consider, for instance, the case of a scientist or philosopher who simultaneously believes in an unreflective way that the car parked outside his office is really yellow (that it does not merely look that way due to the glare of today's unusually bright sunlight, for example) and also in a more reflective way, due to sophisticated scientific or philosophical considerations concerning the status of secondary qualities, suspends belief on the question of whether or not objects such as cars ever really possess secondary qualities such as yellowness. It is not at all clear that either one's attributing to him or his occupying such a divided psychological condition as this need involve any absurdity; for example, it may be that there are two slightly different senses of "believe" or of "really" involved on the two apparently conflicting sides. Now (to come to the point) could not a skeptic about subjective experience, similarly, and likewise without absurdity, both believe in an unreflective way that he possessed such and such current subjective experience and, in his role as skeptic, in a more reflective way suspend belief on that question? Fourth, it seems indicative of the implausibility of this whole argument for thinking a skeptical questioning of one's own current subjective experience impossible that figures such as Democritus and our own modern eliminative materialists have seriously *denied* that there is subjective experience in reality—quite generally, and therefore in their own current cases in particular. For if such serious *denials* are possible, it is surely hard to believe that serious *doubt* is not.[17]

If *Kant* has any argument for his assumption that at least subjective experience is immune to serious skeptical doubt (it is not even entirely clear that he does), then it appears to be a variant of the above argument. For he famously champions the principle of the transcendental unity of apperception: "it must be possible for the 'I think' to accompany all my representations."[18]

This Kantian counterpart to Sextus's and Descartes's principle that current subjective experience necessitates acknowledgment (or belief or knowledge) of it introduces two significant modifications: (1) For Kant, it is not a matter of a necessity that one *actually* acknowledge (or believe or know) one's current subjective experience, but rather of a necessity that one have an *ability* to do so. Hence his circuitous wording: "it must be *possible* for the 'I think' . . ."[19] Hence also his striking position in the *Anthropology* that the bulk of one's subjective experiences are in actuality unconscious.[20] (2) Less importantly for our present purposes, Kant's principle must be understood as restricted in its scope to acknowledgment (or belief or knowledge) of the subject and its subjective experiences *as they appear* rather than *as they are in themselves*.

Despite these significant modifications, Kant's variant of Sextus's and Descartes's argument in the end fares no better than the original, however. The first problem faced by the original version—that the key principle that current subjective experience necessitates acknowledgment (or belief or knowledge) of it can be attacked through skeptical counterargument—has indeed been partially remedied here. For Kant has modified the principle in a way that takes into account the most plausible source of such a counterargument, namely the phenomenon of *unconscious* subjective experience. However, in the course of making that arguable bit of progress on the first problem, he has also considerably exacerbated the third problem—the problem of the illegitimacy of inferring from the necessity of acknowledgment (or belief or knowledge) of current subjective experience to the impossibility of skeptically questioning it. For a skeptic's mere *ability* to acknowledge (or believe or know) his current subjective experience would be an even weaker obstacle to his raising a skeptical doubt about it than his actual acknowledgment (or belief or knowledge) of it would be. Moreover, the second and fourth problems—those concerned with the question-beggingness of the further premise required, and with the phenomenon of actual *denials* of their own current subjective experiences by Democritus and the eliminative materialists— remain just as much in force against a Kantian version of the argument as against Sextus's and Descartes's version of it.

In short, there does in fact seem to be room for raising serious skeptical doubts even about the existence of one's own current subjective experience (and a fortiori about objective experience). Consequently, Kant's strategy of answering skepticism concerning metaphysics by means of transcendental arguments which presuppose that we have experience of certain types, and his conception of his philosophical project as one of investigating problematic synthetic a priori cognition in contrast to supposedly unproblematic synthetic *a posteriori* or experiential knowledge, seem objectionable.

Consider, next, the case of logical principles. This is another area in which Hegel would accuse Kant of having an unacceptably tame conception of Pyrrhonian skepticism's potentials. The neo-Kantian skeptic Schulze, like Kant himself, had considered logical principles invulnerable to skeptical attack.[21] Hegel does not go into this matter in the course of his discussion of Schulze in *The Relation of Skepticism to Philosophy*. But in a roughly contemporary review of a similar position held by Bouterwek he makes it clear that he thinks that a genuine skepticism *will* attack the laws of logic.[22]

Hegel was probably influenced here by an interesting (if at points slightly confused) criticism of Kant for dogmatism in the area of logic developed by a largely forgotten contemporary, C. G. Bardili.[23] As we have seen, Kant had made the question "How is synthetic a priori knowledge possible?" central to his theoretical philosophy, developing elaborate strategies for justifying, and explaining the possibility of, such knowledge. However, he had shown no comparable interest in the question "How is *analytic* a priori knowledge possible?" And this was because he understood analytic propositions to rest solely on the logical law of contradiction, and was satisfied that this and the rest of logic stood in no need of an epistemological investigation because they were "certain entirely a priori,"[24] constituting "a closed and completed body of doctrine" in all essentials unchanged since Aristotle.[25] Bardili took Kant to task for this uncritical reliance on the laws of logic, especially in an essay titled *On Bardili's First, Kant's Transcendental, and the hitherto General Logic*.[26] There, he argued that Kant had left logical laws "merely rhapsodically . . . gathered together"—that is, picked up uncritically from tradition.[27] He noted the oddity of the fact that Kant combined a demand for an investigation of the grounds of possibility of other kinds of knowledge with an entirely uncritical acceptance of logical laws.[28] And, perhaps most interestingly for our present purposes, he pointed out that it appeared to be an assumption underlying Kant's complacency about logical principles that they had not been subjected to any serious skeptical attack, and he questioned the historical accuracy of that assumption.[29]

In both Bardili and Hegel the perception that classical logical principles were vulnerable to skepticism and lacked a sound epistemological defense against it contributed to the inception of a theoretical project of developing a reformed, epistemologically secure logic.[30] We need not concern ourselves with this *positive* side of their positions here. What is relevant for our present purposes is, rather, their shared implications that logic had been subjected to skeptical attacks, that skeptical attacks on it were viable, and that it had not been provided with any adequate epistemological defense against such attacks by Kant or his predecessors. Let us consider each of these implications in turn.

As a matter of history, Hegel and Bardili were certainly right to imply that even the principles of logic had been subjected to skeptical attacks, namely by ancient skeptics. For example, Sextus's texts contain interesting attacks on logical proof.[31] And one of the most impressive attacks on logic is found in Cicero's *Academica*, where the Academic skeptic is represented as (among other things) calling into question the law of bivalence or excluded middle by means of a version of the Liar Paradox: "Clearly it is a fundamental principle of dialectic [i.e., logic] that every statement . . . is either true or false. What then? Is this a true proposition or a false one—'If you say that you are lying and say it truly, you lie'?"[32] The Academic skeptic's point here is that both the assertion that this proposition is true and the assertion that it is false lead to contradiction, which constitutes a ground for classifying it as neither true nor false, contrary to the law of bivalence or excluded middle—so that this consideration can be set against the reasons which we have for *believing* the law of bivalence or excluded middle in order to generate equipollence and hence a suspension of judgment concerning it.

Furthermore, Hegel and Bardili also seem right to imply that such skeptical attacks on classical logic are viable. For example, the attack on the law of bivalence or excluded middle just mentioned is really quite persuasive. And in addition, there have been a considerable number of plausible proposals made in the past (both in a serious and in a more hypothetical spirit) to abandon one or another classical logical law, which the equipollence skeptic might draw on in order to generate a broader balance of arguments for and against particular classical logical laws, thereby motivating suspension of belief concerning them.[33] Using such materials as these, along perhaps with others of his own devising, an equipollence skeptic might, it seems, very well be able to argue to equipollence concerning each classical law of logic, and thereby to motivate a general suspension of belief concerning such laws.[34]

Hegel and Bardili also imply that classical logic has not been provided by Kant or his predecessors with any epistemological defense capable of protecting it against such skeptical attacks. This again appears very plausible.[35]

It might seem that Kant *does* have an effective epistemological defense of classical logic against skepticism, namely the *Critique*'s thesis that general logic "contains the absolutely necessary rules of thought without which there can be no employment whatever of the understanding."[36] For this thesis implies that classical logic enjoys certainty in virtue of the fact that anything that departed from it would simply not be *thought*. Accordingly, Kant writes concerning the law of contradiction in particular that "I can *think* whatever I please, provided only that I do not contradict myself, that is, provided my concept is a possible thought,"[37] and that "the object of a concept which contradicts itself is nothing *because the concept is nothing*."[38] This, then, appears to be Kant's central strategy of epistemological defense.[39]

This strategy of defense was not new with Kant.[40] Aristotle was its original inventor. In *Metaphysics*, book gamma, Aristotle had offered two lines of argument defending classical logical laws against skeptical and other attacks. Taking the law of contradiction as his example, he had argued that (1) it is impossible to believe a contradiction true, and (2) in order to mean or understand anything by words, and hence in order to be capable of thought, one must believe the law of contradiction.[41]

But how plausible are such doctrines? It is important to note, first of all, especially because of the heavy weight of tradition that has built up behind them, and the uncritical presumption in their favor that this can create, that they have little *prima facie* plausibility, even in the case of the law of contradiction (let alone in the case of less fundamental logical principles). This remains true even after one sets aside cases of merely *implicit* self-contradiction, and instead focuses exclusively on *explicit* self-contradictions (as doctrine (1) probably intends). Consider, for instance, the sorts of explicit deviations from and rejections of the law of contradiction that one finds in philosophers such as Heraclitus, Plato, and Engels. Prephilosophically, we are surely strongly inclined to say that these are examples of logically inconsistent *beliefs* and *thoughts* (not non-beliefs and non-thoughts)—no doubt ill justified, false, indeed necessarily false beliefs and thoughts, but *beliefs* and *thoughts* nonetheless.[42]

It would therefore require some sort of non-obvious, compelling *argument* in order to establish such doctrines in the face of our contrary prephilosophical intuitions. Aristotle had attempted to provide such an argument. However, his attempt had not been very successful.

Aristotle's general strategy was to argue at length for (1), and then to infer (2) more or less directly from his case for (1). The latter step might seem very problematic at first sight, but is perhaps not. One apparent problem with it concerns its shift to speaking of conditions of *meaning or understanding*. However, this problem is defused by some of the specific details of Aristotle's case for (1) (see below). Another apparent problem with it concerns what seems to be a crass non sequitur in inferring from people's inability to believe contradictions to their having to believe the law of contradiction.[43] However, this inference may be a reasonable one if, as is likely, what Aristotle has in mind in (2) is *implicit* belief in the law of contradiction. For a person's consistent inability to believe any contradictions, as affirmed by (1), might indeed reasonably be taken to show that he has (or perhaps even must have) an implicit belief in the law of contradiction. Also, just by itself (1) would constitute a pretty strong case for the law of contradiction being in a sense internal to thought. So, in short, we should focus on Aristotle's case for (1).

Aristotle has two main arguments for (1). However, both of them turn out to be deeply problematic on inspection. First, he argues that beliefs in contradictory sentences are themselves contrary properties of a person and therefore cannot both belong to a person at the same time.[44] But this argument just begs the original question, which is in effect precisely whether or not such beliefs *are* contrary properties of a person.[45]

Second, Aristotle argues as follows: In order to mean or understand anything by his words, and hence in order to think (or as Aristotle also vividly puts it, in order to avoid being "like a vegetable"), a person must signify a subject, i.e., a (type of) substance. This requires that he signify some *one* thing, i.e., the essence of a (type of) substance—for example, in the case of the subject "man," "two-footed animal." But to the extent that he also signified the negation of the thing in question—for example, in this case "not a two-footed animal"—he would *fail* to signify one thing.[46]

However, this argument is again problematic. One immediately tempting line of objection to it is of course that it implicitly assumes a highly questionable philosophy of language and metaphysics, including theses to the effect that all meaning or understanding, and hence all thought, must ultimately refer to subjects, or substances, that all substances have essences, that in order to refer to subjects or substances one must signify their essences, and so on. But this sort of objection could perhaps be defused by means of a little reconstruction. In particular, the argument might be recast more simply and plausibly in terms of the somewhat attractive thesis that meaning or understanding any word requires having certain unequivocal analytic beliefs connected with it (e.g., understanding the word "bachelor" requires having an unequivocal belief that all bachelors are unmarried), so that to the extent that one undermined one's claim to possess such unequivocal beliefs by also inclining to believe opposites (e.g., that it is not true that all bachelors are unmarried) one would ipso facto also undermine one's claim to mean or understand words.

A deeper problem with the argument (either in its original or in this reconstructed version) is the following different and more glaring one: Even if the argument were as successful as possible, it would only show that in order to mean or understand anything, and hence in order to think, a person must have *some* beliefs which are not contradictory. But this would fall far short of establishing (1), which says that a person cannot believe *any* contradictions (and would provide no basis at all for inferring (2) either).[47]

Now, when Kant argues in the *Critique* that general logic "contains the absolutely necessary rules of thought without which there can be no employment whatever of the understanding," that "I can *think* whatever I please, provided only that I do not contradict myself, that is, provided my concept is a possible thought," and that "the object of a concept which contradicts itself is nothing *because the concept is nothing*," he does nothing at all to improve this situation. For he is here merely taking over Aristotle's position uncritically and carelessly from tradition, neither clearly recalling its details nor substituting any better ones of his own. This can be seen from the following facts: First, Kant has simply lifted these claims from G. F. Meier's *Vernunftlehre*, the work on which he based his own logic lectures.[48] Second, Kant leaves it unclear whether he is committing himself only to versions of Aristotle's conclusion (1) or also to versions of Aristotle's conclusion (2). Third, Kant neither recalls Aristotle's arguments for (1) and (2) nor substitutes for them any argument of his own, let alone a better one. Instead, he simply advances whichever of these doctrines he means to advance as a sheer dogma.

Furthermore, there are two distinctive features of Kant's version of Aristotle's position which arguably make it even more inferior to Aristotle's version. First, their versions differ in the following respect. Aristotle fundamentally just assumes that the law of contradiction is the most certain of principles, and that it governs all being as such. Accordingly, his arguments for (1) and (2) are not intended to *prove* it, but merely to defend it against deniers.[49] Kant, by contrast, does not fundamentally assume the law to be the most certain principle, or to govern all being as such; rather, for him, the case for (1) (and (2))—such as it is—does constitute a sort of proof of the law, one which is supposed to establish, not only its necessity for thought, but also, and thereby, its necessity, if not for being, then for truth, namely on the grounds that any violation of it would destroy the thought whose correspondence to an object constitutes truth according to Kant's standard correspondence theory of truth.[50] Now the arguable further disadvantage for Kant that arises from this difference is not so much that he is staking everything on the case in question, whereas Aristotle is not— for it is not really clear that Aristotle's dogmatic starting point is superior to a less dogmatic one based on an inadequate argument. Rather, it is that even if Kant could establish (1) (and (2)), and thereby establish that all thought, and hence also all truth in the sense of a correspondence between thought and object, must conform to the law of contradiction, that would still leave open the question whether all *being* must do so.

Second, Kant's commitment to his position that general logic "contains the absolutely necessary rules of thought without which there can be no employment whatever of the understanding" involves an implicit incoherence. His adoption of this position is motivated not *only* by his desire to ensure logic's epistemological security, but also by a desire to account for its *necessity*. The latter project is prompted by an implicit assumption which he makes to the effect that all modal facts (i.e., in this context, all necessities and possibilities) must ultimately be reducible to, or explicable in terms of, *non*-modal ones, actualities.[51] What non-modal fact constitutes the necessity of the principles of general logic? Answer: Their being constitutive of the very nature of thought. However, there is a problem here which Kant overlooks, namely that this explanation *itself implicitly includes a modal claim*: as he himself puts it in the quotation above, "without which there *can* be no . . ." Indeed, the explanation *must* do so in order to avoid collapsing into a type of psychologism about logic which Kant himself strongly opposes.[52] This shows that the explanation cannot, at least as it stands, satisfy the aforementioned assumption which largely motivated Kant to offer it in the first place.[53]

In sum, Kant has no better epistemological defense of classical logic to offer than Aristotle. Rather, the contrary.

Furthermore, even if Aristotle and Kant's doctrines (1) and (2) *were* correct, they would constitute a much weaker epistemological defense of classical logic than the two philosophers suppose. The later Wittgenstein saw the Achilles' heel here. He was himself sometimes prepared to endorse at least doctrines of sort (1). For example, in the *Remarks on the Foundations of Mathematics* he writes that the classical laws of logic "can be said to show: how human beings think, and also *what* human beings call 'thinking.' "[54] However, he was not at all inclined to see this (alleged) situation as a sufficient reason for considering the classical laws of logic beyond question. For he recognized that even if this situation obtained, there might still be something *similar* to what we call thought (or propositions, etc.) of which adherence to one or more of the classical laws was *not* an essential ingredient as it seems to be an essential ingredient of what we call that, but which was nevertheless as good and useful an instrument as what we call that, or perhaps even a better, more useful one. One of his pithiest expressions of such a line of argument occurs not in relation to logical laws themselves but in relation to the (in his view) analogous case of mathematical laws: "I could imagine . . . that people had a different calculus, or a technique which we should not call 'calculating.' But would it be *wrong*?"[55] Accordingly, when he considers Russell's Paradox in the *Remarks on the Foundations of Mathematics* he in effect concedes to the Aristotle-Kant tradition that what we call propositions are *essentially* used in conformity with the law of contradiction, but this does not at all prevent him from raising the possibility that it might be sensible in this case to violate the law: "Why should Russell's contradiction not be conceived as something supra-propositional, something that towers above the propositions and looks in both directions like a Janus head? . . . Might one not even begin logic with this contradiction? And as it were descend from it to propositions."[56]

Hegel too recognized this Achilles' heel in the Aristotle-Kant tradition's defense of classical logic. Thus, on the one hand, like Wittgenstein, Hegel was often inclined to concede to that tradition that classical logic was an essential ingredient of what we usually call thought, or of what he himself calls the thought of the *Understanding*.[57] But on the other hand, again like Wittgenstein, he also affirmed the possibility that there might be a different kind of "thought" of which classical logic was *not* an essential ingredient, but which was nevertheless as good and useful an instrument, or even a better, more useful one. Indeed, he believed that such an alternative was not only possible but really available, and not merely as good but superior—and he called this the thought of *Reason*.

In short, as in the case of subjective (and a fortiori, objective) experience, it seems that there *is* in fact room for serious Pyrrhonian skeptical doubts concerning logic after all. Consequently, Kant's strategy of defending metaphysics against skepticism by means of transcendental arguments which presuppose the certainty of logic, and his fundamental conception of his philosophical project as an epistemological inquiry into a synthetic a priori knowledge which he assumes to be problematic in contrast to analytic a priori, or logically based, knowledge which he assumes to be unproblematic, in the end seem objectionable.

In sum, Kant's project of addressing skepticism about metaphysics seems open to criticism for failing to take the more radical potentials of Pyrrhonian skepticism sufficiently into account.

Notes

1. Kant's preoccupation with skepticism is hardly news, being a staple component of almost all recent Anglophone interpretations of Kant for example. But this further point is much more controversial, contradicting most of those interpretations for example.

2. Again, Kant's central preoccupation with reforming metaphysics is hardly news in itself; it has been emphasized especially in the German literature (notably by H. Heimsoeth and M. Heidegger), but also by others (e.g., H. J. de Vleeschauwer and D. P. Dryer). However, the further point made here is more controversial (sharply contradicting the anti-epistemological readings of Heimsoeth and Heidegger, for example).

3. It will seem less heretical—though not, I hope, merely orthodox—to scholars in the German tradition. For example, my devaluation of "veil of perception" skepticism agrees with H. Heimsoeth's reading, and my accentuation of Pyrrhonism coheres to a significant extent with positions argued for by B. Erdmann, G. Tonelli, and N. Hinske.

4. Certain aspects of this part of my account will be at least roughly familiar from existing secondary literature. Others will be altogether unfamiliar. One example of the latter: an anti-skeptical motive and function which I shall be ascribing to the systematic, or "architectonic," character of Kant's reformed metaphysics.

CHAPTER TWO
"VEIL OF PERCEPTION" SKEPTICISM

1. Two recent examples—both in many ways excellent philosophers, incidentally—are Paul Guyer and Barry Stroud. For instance, Guyer claims in this vein that "Kant clearly conceived of the problem of knowledge in terms of methodological solipsism. That is, like thinkers from Descartes to Hume, he supposed that an answer to skepticism must lie in what reflection on his own thoughts can reveal to the individual thinker even on the supposition that nothing but his own consciousness exists" (P. Guyer, review of D. Henrich, *Identität und Objektivität*, in *Journal of Philosophy*, no. 76 [1979]; cf. his *Kant and the Claims of Taste* [Cambridge, Mass.: Harvard University Press, 1979], pp. 288–91; *Kant and the Claims of Knowledge* [Cambridge: Cambridge University Press, 1987], pp. 75, 207–8, 252–6, 279; such an assumption leads almost inevitably to Guyer's position in *Kant and the Claims of Knowledge* that the Refutation of Idealism constitutes the real heart of the *Critique*). For Stroud's similar picture, see B. Stroud, *The Significance of Philosophical Scepticism* (Oxford: Clarendon Press, 1984), ch. 4; and "Kant and Skepticism," in *The Skeptical Tradition*, ed. M. F. Burnyeat (Berkeley: University of California Press, 1983).

2. H. Heimsoeth seems to me essentially correct when he argues concerning Kant that "the grounds for the formation of the concept of the thing in itself and the limitation of our objective cognition to appearances which were earliest and then remained constantly in effect are not 'epistemological' in an introspective-reflexive, phenomenological, or indeed psychological . . . sense of the word . . . In contrast to later idealistic lines of thought which begin from *consciousness* and consider that they thence prove the assumption of a thing in itself transcendent of consciousness to be a 'non-thought,' Kant sees no difficulty in the transition from being into consciousness, and particularly in the impact of existing substances on existing intelligences (which thereby have direct experience of properties of those external substances). For him the riddle lies solely in the synthetic a priori aspects of our cognition of reality" ("Metaphysische Motive in der Ausbildung des kritischen Idealismus," *Kant Studien*, vol. 29 [1924], pp. 121–2).

3. It is of some symptomatic significance for my overall thesis in this essay—and also important for interpreting the texts correctly—that Kant hardly ever refers to "veil of perception" skepticism as "skepticism" simpliciter, instead reserving this designation for Humean skepticism and Pyrrhonian equipollence skepticism. (There

are occasional exceptions to this rule, e.g., *Mrongovius Metaphysics*, AA 29[1,2]:927.)

4. *Critique*, Bxxxix.

5. AA 1:410, proposition 12.

6. AA 1:411.

7. There are a few minor exceptions. For example, there is a brief attempt to dispel this sort of skepticism in the *Inaugural Dissertation* of 1770, at AA 2:397, par. 11. Again, one can see from Herder's *Versuch über das Sein*, written under the immediate influence of Kant's metaphysics lectures in the early 1760s, that Kant had been discussing this sort of skepticism—as the problem of "egoism" or "idealism"—in his lectures at this period (*Johann Gottfried Herder Werke*, ed. U. Gaier et al. [Frankfurt am Main: Deutscher Klassiker Verlag, 1985–], 1:10–11, 17, 19, 21). Again, there are a few brief and undeveloped private notes by Kant plausibly assignable to the period in question which allude to this sort of skepticism (see esp. AA 17, no. 4445; also *Reflexionen Kants zur Kritik der reinen Vernunft*, ed. B. Erdmann [Leipzig: Fues's Verlag, 1884], no. 1167; cf. nos. 1165–9). But not much more.

8. For example, in the *Blomberg Logic* from 1771 Kant writes of Pyrrho in a spirit of defense: "People . . . blamed Pyrrho for doubting the truth of all empirical judgments. However, this is a pure invention which has no basis at all" (AA 24:214).

9. AA 4:260–2. Cf. *Critique*, B5, B19–20, B127–8 (comparing A112–13, B168), A760–9 / B788–97; *Critique of Practical Reason*, AA 5:50–6.

10. For example, A. C. Ewing, *Kant's Treatment of Causality* (London: Routledge and Kegan Paul, 1924), esp. pp. 6–15, 47; P. F. Strawson, *The Bounds of Sense* (London: Methuen, 1966), pp. 18–19, 88.

11. Hume, *An Enquiry concerning the Human Understanding*, sec. 12.

12. Thus in the *Critique of Practical Reason*, recounting his own debt to Hume's skepticism concerning causation, Kant says: "I granted that *when Hume took the objects of experience as things in themselves (as is almost always done)*, he was entirely correct in declaring the concept of cause to be deceptive and an illusion" (p. 53, emphasis added; H. E. Allison's claim at *Kant's Transcendental Idealism* [New Haven: Yale University Press, 1983], p. 18 that Kant here only means that Hume assumed the subject's own *mental states* to be things in themselves seems impossibly forced). Cf. F. C. Beiser, *German Idealism* (Cambridge, Mass.: Harvard University Press, 2002), pp. 43–5.

13. *Critique*, A177 / B218. Occasional exceptions to this rule occur, e.g., in the Refutation of Idealism at B275–8, and later at A343 / B401: "inner experience."

14. See ibid., A107: "There can be in us no modes of cognition . . . without that unity of consciousness which precedes all data of intuitions, and by relation to which representation of objects is alone possible" (cf. A110, 113, 115–16).

15. See esp. ibid., A92–4 / B125–6; cf. A96, 109–10, 115, 119–20; B130, 137, 145–7.

16. See, e.g., ibid., B233–4, A195 / B240, A201–2 / B246–7.

17. Ibid., Bxxxix–xli.

18. AA 18, nos. 5461, 5653–5, 5709, 6311–17, 6323.

19. It merely makes a brief appearance at *Prolegomena*, pp. 336–7, where Kant anticipates the Refutation of Idealism of the second-edition *Critique*.

20. Kant's letters from the relevant period rarely touch on this sort of skepticism, and when they do, tend to be hastily dismissive of it (see, e.g., the letter to J. S. Beck of December 4, 1792, in *Emmanuel Kant: Philosophical Correspondence 1759–99* [henceforth: *Philosophical Correspondence*], tr. A. Zweig [Chicago: The University of Chicago Press, 1986], p. 198). His *Reflexionen* concerning it from the period—especially AA 18, nos. 5461, 5653–5, 5709, 6311–17, and 6323—are more substantial, but hardly numerous in relation to his output, and hardly central (the lowly position and little weight that he accords it in his sketch "Von der Veranlassung der Kritik" in no. 6317 are revealing). His lectures on metaphysics from the period touch on it at a few points, but again not extensively or centrally (see, e.g., AA 28[2,1]:680, 725, 770–3). Finally, his formal writings virtually ignore it.

21. Kant's own position in the Refutation of Idealism is in a way similar to the position I am advocating here, since he too thinks that one's beliefs about one's own subjective mental states are *no more* certain than one's beliefs about the mind-external world (a stance which also emerges at other points in the *Critique*, e.g., in the Transcendental Deduction at A108, and later on at B291–4). However, he thinks them *both certain*—if not individually, then at least as groups—whereas I am inclined to see them both as vulnerable to skeptical attack.

22. The following are some points to note in this connection. Concerning the Fourth Paralogism, Kant's strategy there of answering the "veil of perception" skeptic by means of a phenomenalistic reduction of objects to representations confronts at least two immediate problems: (1) There is the internal problem that—even in the first edition, let alone in the second—Kant's official view is that phenomenalism is only true with the considerable qualification that "represen-

tation in itself does not produce its object insofar as its *existence* is concerned" (A92, cf. A104–5), but of course for the "veil of perception" skeptic it is above all precisely the *existence* of mind-external objects that is in question. (It seems to me likely that Kant lost faith in the Fourth Paralogism by the time of the second edition largely for just this reason.) (2) In order to be even remotely plausible as a thesis, a phenomenalistic reduction of objects to representations would need to reduce them to representations *from different times*, but—as Descartes had already hinted in the Second Meditation ("This proposition 'I am,' 'I exist,' *whenever I utter it or conceive it in my mind*, is true"; "I am, I exist; that is certain. For how long? *For as long as I am experiencing*"; "It is just not possible, *when I see or . . . I think I see*, that my conscious self should not be something" [*Descartes: Philosophical Writings* [Norwich: Thomas Nelson, 1971], pp. 67, 69, 74; emphasis added])—any "veil of perception" skeptic worth his salt will restrict the mental states concerning which he grants a person certain knowledge to the *present time* only.

Again, the Refutation of Idealism faces at least the following two problems: (3) In its central formulation it depends on doctrines borrowed from the First Analogy which seem very dubious—specifically, concerning the imperceptibility of time, and the consequent need for a perceptible analogon of permanent time in the form of substance. (4) To the extent that we search in the text for a more plausible line of argument which could dispense with those dubious assumptions, we encounter serious problems in connection with Kant's highly ambiguous premise that "I am conscious of my own existence as determined in time." In order to generate a plausible argument that such consciousness presupposes knowledge of something outside of one, we would need to construe this premise either as concerned with one's knowing *objective dates* of one's mental states (e.g., January 29, 2007 at 11 p.m.), in which case no sensible "veil of perception" skeptic will concede it, or as concerned with one's knowing that one has had mental states in a certain order *over a stretch of time*, in which case the problem already indicated in (2) arises, namely that no "veil of perception" skeptic worth his salt will concede this claim either. By contrast, such a skeptic might well be prepared to concede that one knows that one is in such and such a mental state or states *now* (a third possible reading of the premise). But then, how is Kant going to argue plausibly from *that* concession to one's knowledge of something outside oneself?

CHAPTER THREE
SKEPTICISM AND METAPHYSICS (A PUZZLE)

1. Cf. W. H. Walsh, *Reason and Experience* (Oxford: Clarendon Press, 1947), pp. 130, 238–9.

2. See M. Wundt, *Die deutsche Schulmetaphysik des 17. Jahrhunderts* (Hildesheim: Georg Olms, 1992), *Die deutsche Schulphilosophie im Zeitalter der Aufklärung* (Hildesheim: Georg Olms, 1964).

3. Concerning this conception of metaphysics within the Wolffian tradition and Kant's relation to it, see H. J. de Vleeschauwer, "Wie ich jetzt die *Kritik der reinen Vernunft* entwicklungsgeschichtlich lese," *Kant Studien*, vol. 54, no. 4 (1963). For an example of the precritical Kant's own commitment to such a two-part metaphysics, see his *Notice concerning the Structure of Lectures in the Winter Semester* 1765–1766, at AA 2:308–10. One anomaly should perhaps be mentioned: Wolff and Baumgarten had both included within special metaphysics an *empirical* as well as a rational psychology (Kant himself identifies this as an anomaly at AA 20:281; cf. *Critique*, A848–9 / B876–7).

4. *Critique*, A761 / B789: "The first step in matters of pure reason, marking its infancy, is *dogmatic*. The second step is *skeptical* . . . But a third step, such as can be taken only by fully matured judgment . . . is now necessary . . . This is . . . the *criticism* of reason."

5. *Prolegomena*, p. 260. Cf. *Critique*, A760–8 / B788–96.

6. *Philosophical Correspondence*, p. 252.

7. "This is indeed puzzling. Can it be due to a lapse of memory? The letter is filled with complaints about Kant's declining health and mental abilities" (L. W. Beck, *Essays on Kant and Hume* [New Haven: Yale University Press, 1978], p. 119).

8. *Prize Essay*, AA 20:319–20: "Another strange phenomenon in the end inevitably startled awake the Reason which was slumbering on the pillow of the cognition which it supposed itself to have extended beyond all bounds of possible experience by ideas, and that is the discovery that . . . those [a priori propositions] which overstep the bounds of possible experience . . . come into conflict, partly among themselves, partly with those [a priori propositions] which are concerned with knowledge of nature, and seem to destroy one another, but thereby to rob reason of all confidence in the theoretical field, and to introduce a boundless skepticism. Against this disaster there is, now, no remedy but to subject Reason itself, i.e., the faculty of a priori cognition generally, to an exact and detailed critique." Cf. *Critique*, A407 / B433–4, A757 / B785.

CHAPTER FOUR
KANT'S PYRRHONIAN CRISIS

1. It is characteristic of the *Critique*'s Antinomies that "thesis, as well as antithesis, can be shown by equally convincing, clear, and irresistible proofs" (*Prolegomena*, p. 340).

2. In the *Critique* the first two Antinomies are concerned with the world as a whole, the third Antinomy with the human soul, and the fourth Antinomy with God (though Kant also tends to think of them *all* as concerned with the world as a whole).

3. *Philosophical Correspondence*, p. 97; emphasis added. Lambert's original letter making his proposal has survived (see ibid., pp. 46–7).

4. The First Antinomy—the world has a beginning in time and limits in space vs. it has no beginning and no limits—is not found in Kant's own writings from the period in question, but its spatial version had already been published by Crusius in the 1740s (see L. W. Beck, *Early German Philosophy* [Cambridge, Mass.: Harvard University Press, 1969], pp. 399–400) and would therefore certainly have been familiar to Kant. Famously, an early version of the Second Antinomy—all composite substances are made up of simple parts vs. none are—is already found in Kant's *Physical Monadology* of 1756 (where he sets philosophy's denial of the infinite divisibility of space and mathematics' affirmation of this into opposition to one another). A version of the Third Antinomy—there is a causality of freedom vs. there is only thoroughgoing causality in accordance with the laws of nature—had already been developed by Crusius in the 1740s (see Beck, *Early German Philosophy*, p. 400), and though it was at first countered by Kant with a compatibilist argument in the *New Elucidation* of 1755, it was subsequently taken much more seriously by him in *The Only Possible Argument in Support of a Demonstration of God's Existence* of 1763, where he pruned back his initial claim of compatibility to a claim that the causality of freedom is not *entirely* emancipated from the laws of nature, and says that the nature of the causality of freedom is not properly understood (AA 2:110–11). Finally, concern about a version of the Fourth Antinomy—there is an absolutely necessary being vs. there is none (only a chain of contingent causes)—already lies behind Kant's argument in the *Universal Natural History and Theory of the Heavens* of 1755 for nature being thoroughly explicable in terms of natural laws and for this being not only compatible with God's design of the world, but actually indicative of it, and better in keeping with it than a restriction of the applicability of natural laws within nature (this is a sort of counterpart to Kant's compatibilist argument concerning human

freedom from the *New Elucidation* of the same year). Concerning the precritical Kant's anticipations of the four Antinomies of the *Critique*, cf. N. Hinske, *Kants Weg zur Transzendentalphilosophie* (Stuttgart: Kohlhammer, 1970).

5. As Hinske notes—ibid., pp. 95–6—this only happened later. It began in the *Inaugural Dissertation* of 1770, where Kant for the first time brought together the first two Antinomies (the third and the fourth were added to the system still later).

6. For example, in the *Physical Monadology* of 1756 Kant mentions not only an early version of the Second Antinomy but also several other antinomies which do not belong to the canonical four: "How to reconcile metaphysics, which denies that space is infinitely divisible, with geometry, which asserts it with certitude? [This is Kant's early version of the Second Antinomy.—M.N.F.] Geometry contends that empty space is necessary for free motion, metaphysics denies it. Geometry holds universal attraction or gravitation to be hardly explicable by mechanical causes, but shows clearly that it comes from forces inherent in bodies at rest and acting at a distance; metaphysics renounces this as an imaginary plaything" (AA 1:475–6). Another example of noncanonical antinomies is provided by *Dreams of a Spirit Seer, Illustrated by Dreams of Metaphysics* from 1766, namely in its reflections on the philosophy of mind. Concerning the whole question of further antinomies, cf. Hinske, *Kants Weg zur Transzendentalphilosophie*, pp. 95–6.

7. Sextus Empiricus, *Outlines of Pyrrhonism* (Cambridge, Mass.: Harvard University Press, 1976), bk. 1, sec. 12 (translation slightly amended): "The main basic principle of the skeptic system is that of opposing to every proposition/argument [*logos*] an equal proposition/argument; for we believe that as a consequence of this we end by ceasing to dogmatize."

8. *Critique*, A388–9.

9. AA 2:306–7.

10. The term "zetetic" is one distinctively used by the Pyrrhonists to characterize themselves and this procedure of theirs (see, for example, *Outlines of Pyrrhonism*, bk. 1, sec. 7: "The skeptic school, then, is also called zetetic [*zêtetikê*] from its activity in investigation [*to zêtein*] and inquiry"). In a letter to Mendelssohn roughly contemporary with the *Notice* Kant advocates what is obviously the same thing as the "zetetic" method referred to in the latter as a method of treating metaphysics' "pretended insights *skeptically*" (*Philosophical Correspondence*, p. 55; emphasis added). In some roughly contemporary notes written into his copy of his own work *Observations on the Feeling of the Beautiful and the Sublime* he states concerning metaphysics: "The doubt that I accept

is . . . a doubt of postponement. Zetetici (*zêtein*), Seekers. I shall accentuate the grounds belonging to both sides" (AA 20:175). Again, if further evidence were needed, in the *Blomberg Logic* of 1771 Kant notes that the Pyrrhonists describe themselves as "zetetici" (pp. 36, 213), and in *Reflexionen* from the 1770s he uses the same adjective to characterize the method of balancing opposed arguments (AA 17, nos. 4454–5). Concerning the adjective's reference to Pyrrhonism in the passage quoted in my main text, cf. G. Tonelli, "Kant und die antiken Skeptiker," in *Studien zu Kants philosophischer Entwicklung*, ed. H. Heimsoeth et al. (Hildesheim: Georg Olms, 1967), pp. 94–6. In seeing the adjective as referring more specifically to the Pyrrhonists' equipollence method I go beyond Tonelli, however (contrast ibid., p. 121, n. 98).

11. Observe in particular that the *Notice* still only envisaged applying the zetetic method to metaphysics as a means to *discovering truth* in the discipline, not yet as a means to destroying it, for the text says that the method's catharsis will lead to a metaphysics which "becomes . . . in various parts *dogmatic*, that is decided" (AA 2:307).

12. To illustrate the fundamental role that the application of this method to metaphysics plays in *Dreams of a Spirit Seer* (since this may not be immediately obvious from the text): (1) That role is evident from Kant's explicit comments there on his approach to metaphysical questions. For example, he writes, "I am sufficiently sure of myself not to fear any opponent, no matter how dreadful his weapons may be . . . so that I can in this case test argument against argument in refutation, for among men of learning such testing is really the art of demonstrating each other's ignorance" (AA 2:328). (2) It is also evident from his practice in the text of actually arguing on both sides of metaphysical questions in order to motivate suspension of judgment. In particular, after opening with some remarks which call the very *concept* of "spirit" into question (p. 320 ff.)—incidentally, an opening move that is typical of Sextus Empiricus, who often prefaces an equipollence argument in this way—he goes on to develop an argument which is generally supportive of a view like Swedenborg's concerning the relation between a world of spirits and the world of material phenomena (pp. 322–41), but then turns round and argues against any such view, instead offering a physiological explanation of its delusiveness (pp. 342–8), and finally concludes with the moral that we are ignorant about such matters (pp. 349–52). (3) It is because of his conviction that this method can always be deployed successfully against supersensuous metaphysics that he argues in the essay that the judgments of supersensuous metaphysics are irremediably subjective rather than intersubjective, and consequently nothing more than a kind of dream: "dreams of reason," no

better than the sensuous illusions, or "dreams of sensation," of the seer Swedenborg when he claims direct acquaintance with a spiritual realm unrecognized by the rest of us (p. 342). For Kant's thought here, to unpack it a little, is as follows. He is assuming that intersubjectivity in judgments is a necessary condition of their constituting objective cognitions rather than merely expressing a subject's own mental states ("It seems to me that one ought, perhaps . . . to say: if different people have each of them their own world, then we may suppose that they are dreaming" [p. 342]; incidentally, this assumption subsequently survives to play an important role in Kant's critical period). And he thinks that the equal balance of opposed arguments in supersensuous metaphysics which is uncovered by the zetetic or equipollence method ensures that judgments in the discipline are merely subjective rather than intersubjective, because it leaves, not rational arguments, but instead non-rational inclinations as the ultimate determinants of belief within the discipline, and these, unlike decisive rational arguments, are variable from individual to individual (pp. 349–51).

13. "Previously we moved like Democritus in empty space where the butterfly wings of metaphysics had carried us and we conversed there with spiritual forms. Now that the contracting power of self-knowledge has drawn together metaphysics' silken wings, we find ourselves on the lowly ground of experience and the common understanding; fortunate! if we regard this ground as our appointed place, which we can never leave without paying the penalty" (ibid., p. 368).

14. Ibid., pp. 306–8, 342, 368–72 (empirical disciplines and mathematics); pp. 311, 334–5, 372 (first-order moral judgments); p. 310 (common logic). (Moral *philosophy* and more ambitious forms of logic are another matter—see pp. 308, 310–11.)

15. Ibid., p. 367.

16. This move had precedents among some of Kant's skeptically minded modern predecessors. See Tonelli, "Kant und die antiken Skeptiker," pp. 107–8.

17. Pace Tonelli, ibid., p. 110. Tonelli mistakenly takes a contrary view because he underestimates both (1) the distinctiveness of *Dreams of a Spirit Seer* in comparison with previous works by Kant and (2) the moderateness of orthodox Pyrrhonism as Kant interprets it.

18. More exactly, it is precisely the estimation belonging to what Kant considers the superior orthodox Pyrrhonism of Pyrrho himself, as opposed to what Kant considers the inferior excessive skepticism propounded by some later Pyrrhonists and Academic skeptics (*Blomberg Logic*, pp. 210, 213–16).

19. On the one hand: "People . . . blamed Pyrrho for doubting the truth of all *empirical* judgments and not placing faith in them. However, this is a pure invention which has no basis at all" (ibid., p. 214, emphasis added); "Pyrrho: that general dogmata (except for *mathematics*) were uncertain" (*Herder Logic*, AA 24:4, emphasis added); "That [Pyrrho] rejected each and every dogma is fundamentally mistaken. One who accepts no dogmas at all cannot teach *morality* at all" (*Blomberg Logic*, p. 214, emphasis added); for Pyrrho "there are certain, so to speak, eternal principles of our reason [i.e. *logic* and mathematics—M.N.F.], which cannot be disputed at all" (ibid., p. 214). On the other hand: "[Pyrrho] taught only that one ought not to accept and decide on the propositions of philosophy straight away but should begin by doubting them" (*Philippi Logic*, AA 24:330), and "it is beyond doubt that he particularly rejected many rational judgments" (*Blomberg Logic*, pp. 213-14).

20. *Dreams of a Spirit Seer*, pp. 318, 368 (the useful); 368, 373 (happiness); 338-9, 351, 362-3 (life).

21. In thus accounting for Kant's skepticism about metaphysics in *Dreams of a Spirit Seer* as primarily Pyrrhonian in character and inspiration, I am somewhat at odds with K. Fischer, who argues at *Immanuel Kant und seine Lehre* (Heidelberg: Carl Winter, 1889), pt. 1, pp. 265-73 that the skepticism which underlies the essay is Humean skepticism. Favoring my reading over Fischer's, note, in addition to the evidence already presented, also the following fact: Just a few years after *Dreams of a Spirit Seer*, in the *Blomberg Logic* of 1771, Kant gives an extended and highly sympathetic account of Pyrrhonism (pp. 4, 36, 207-18), whereas by contrast his discussion of Hume is brief, critical, poorly informed, and moreover interprets Hume as in effect merely a sort of inferior Pyrrhonist—in particular, as a skeptic who uses the method of balancing opposed arguments (which he does not) in order to arrive at an unrestricted and therefore excessive doubt (pp. 210-11, 217). However, my disagreement with Fischer is not as sharp as it may seem at this point, for I would allow that Hume's influence is at work in the essay alongside Pyrrhonism's (especially in connection with the essay's thesis that particular causal connections and laws cannot be known a priori but only on the basis of experience—concerning which more later).

22. *Critique*, Aviii. Cf. B22-3: reason's "dogmatic employment . . . lands us in dogmatic assertions to which other assertions, equally specious, can always be opposed—that is, in *skepticism*."

23. *Prolegomena*, pp. 255, 271 (the historical allusion here is of course to ancient skepticism). Cf. *Prize Essay*, p. 263; and Kant's lec-

tures on metaphysics from the critical period, which contain numerous similar statements, e.g., at AA 28(1):362, 378; 28(2,1):618–21; 29(1,2):752, 779–80, 955–8.

24. For example, compare with the passage just quoted from the first edition of the *Critique*, A421–5 / B448–53 in the same work.

25. Passages such as the following might be cited in support of such a proposal: "There are just so many, neither more nor fewer" (ibid., A462 / B490).

26. See ibid., A395 / B417–18, note b; A701–2 / B729–30; A741 / B769. Cf. Kant's encouragement of a broad "defensive" use of the equipollence method in relation to metaphysics at A776–82 / B804–10.

27. See *Critique of Practical Reason*, pp. 113 ff.; *Critique of Judgment*, AA 5:338 ff., 385 ff.; *Religion within the Limits of Reason Alone*, AA 6: 116 ff.

CHAPTER FIVE
HUMEAN SKEPTICISM

1. *Critique*, A760–8 / B788–96.

2. Hume, *Enquiry*, sec. 4, pt. 1. Thus Kant writes: "[Hume] demonstrated irrefutably that it was entirely impossible for reason to think such a connection a priori and by means of concepts . . . We cannot at all see how, in consequence of the existence of one thing, another must necessarily exist, and how therefore the conception of such a connection can be introduced a priori" (*Prolegomena*, p. 257; cf. *Critique*, A765–6 / B793–4).

3. Hume, *Enquiry*, sec. 7. Thus Kant writes: "[Hume] concluded that reason deceives itself entirely in this concept, that . . . it is in fact nothing but a mongrel of the imagination which, impregnated by experience, has brought certain representations under the law of association and substitutes a subjective necessity which arises thereby, that is, custom, for an objective necessity arising from insight" (*Prolegomena*, pp. 257–8). Cf. *Critique*, B127, A760 / B788; *Critique of Practical Reason*, pp. 50–1. Also, *Volckmann Metaphysics*, AA 28(1):403–4: "Hume . . . based a whole skeptical philosophy on the question: how do you arrive at the concept of cause? A cause is that which contains the real ground for something's existence and is quite one with the real ground, for example the wind is the cause of the ship's motion. How can it be, then, that when you posit the wind, at the same time something quite

different follows as well, namely the motion of the ship? What sort of connection has the wind with the motion? According to him, all concepts of cause and effect are got from experience, and *necessity*, he says, is merely something imagined and a long habit. Hence he saw no other way, since he could not derive the relation from reason, than to assume the concept of the real ground to be an empirical concept."

4. Hume, *A Treatise of Human Nature* (henceforth: *Treatise*), bk. 1, sec. 3. The *Prolegomena*'s opening discussion of Hume's reminder refers to this third Humean view only obliquely, but its central importance for Kant is clear from later parts of the *Prolegomena* (in particular, secs. 27–30), and from corresponding passages in the *Critique* (B4–5, B19–20, A760 / B788, A765–6 / B793–4).

L. W. Beck and others have indeed seen this Humean view concerning the causal principle as *the* Humean catalyst in Kant's awakening from his dogmatic slumber in metaphysics (*Essays on Kant and Hume*, pp. 117–20). However, I hope to show that that is an oversimplification.

5. *Dreams of a Spirit Seer*, p. 370: "The rules of reason concern only comparison with respect to identity and contradiction. But in the case of a cause something is assumed to have come from something else, so that one can find no connection with respect to identity. Similarly, if I want to postulate that the same thing is not a cause, a contradiction never results, because no contradiction arises if one postulates something but does away with something else. Therefore our fundamental concepts of things as causes . . . are absolutely arbitrary and can be neither proved nor disproved unless they are derived from experience." It would be perverse to deny Hume's role in influencing Kant to accept this doctrine in *Dreams of a Spirit Seer*, as Erdmann did— B. Erdmann, *Reflexionen Kants zur Kritik der reinen Vernunft*, pp. xxi ff., lff., and "Kant und Hume um 1762," pts. 1 and 2, *Archiv für Geschichte der Philosophie*, vol. 1 (1887–8). (1) By the time Kant wrote the passage just quoted in 1766 Hume's *Enquiry* had been available to him in German translation for over ten years; we have ample evidence of his reading Hume in the intervening period (e.g., Herder, who attended Kant's lectures in the early 1760s, notes in his *Briefe zu Beförderung der Humanität* that Hume was one of the most frequently cited authors, and Hume is explicitly referred to in connection with practical philosophy in Kant's *Notice* of 1765); and, as we have seen, the *Prolegomena* acknowledges the doctrine's indebtedness to Hume about as prominently and explicitly as one could wish. (2) The case for Hume's influence is, moreover, reinforced by the fact that *Dreams of a Spirit Seer* contains, immediately following the passage just quoted, a further pas-

sage on the subject of causation—specifically, concerning the causal influence of the will on the body—which is so similar in both argument and illustrative details to a passage from the *Enquiry* on the same subject that it seems virtually inconceivable that it was written without that passage in mind. Kant's passage reads: "I know to be sure that thought and volition move my body, but I can never reduce this appearance as a simple experience to another through analysis, so that I can certainly recognize it but not understand it. That my will moves my arm is no more intelligible to me than if someone were to say that the will could also control the moon in its orbit; the difference is only this: that I experience the former but the latter has never occurred to my senses" (p. 370). Compare with this the following passage from the *Enquiry*: "Is there any principle in all nature more mysterious than the union of soul with body; by which a supposed spiritual substance acquires such an influence over a material one, that the most refined thought is able to actuate the grossest matter? Were we empowered, by a secret wish, to remove mountains, or control planets in their orbit; this extensive authority would not be more extraordinary, nor more beyond our comprehension" (sec. 7, pt. 1). Erdmann's attempt—"Kant und Hume um 1762," pt. 2, pp. 218–19—to dismiss the resemblance between these passages as merely coincidental is surely very implausible; and his claim in support of this dismissal that there is nothing that makes the hypothesis of an influence of Hume on Kant in *Dreams of a Spirit Seer* "secured elsewhere [*anderweitig gesichert*]," unless it presupposes an *absurdly* high standard for evidence, is simply false, due to the remarks on particular causal judgments in *Dreams of a Spirit Seer* and the *Prolegomena* which we have just considered, and also the presence of moral reflections in a Humean spirit at the end of *Dreams of a Spirit Seer* (pp. 372–3) shortly after Kant had explicitly praised Hume's moral philosophy in the *Notice* (p. 311). (3) None of this need be to deny that influences *other* than Hume were *also* pushing Kant's views on the subject of particular causal judgments in the direction of the position found in *Dreams of a Spirit Seer*—as has been plausibly suggested by L. W. Beck, and especially G. Tonelli ("Die Anfänge von Kants Kritik der Kausalbeziehungen und ihre Voraussetzungen im 18. Jahrhundert," *Kant Studien*, vol. 57 [1966]).

6. *Dreams of a Spirit Seer*, pp. 370–1; *Philosophical Correspondence*, pp. 55–7.

7. See, for example, the *Physical Monadology* of 1756, at AA 1:475, and the *Inquiry concerning the Distinctness of the Principles of Natural Theology and Morality* from 1764, at AA 2:286.

8. Further Humean influences on *Dreams of a Spirit Seer* are likely as well. In addition to those already mentioned in my main text and in note 5, plausible candidates are passages which suggest that all of our concepts must be empirical (pp. 322, 367–8) and passages which confine our non-mathematical, non-logical, non-moral knowledge to experience (pp. 351–2, 368 ff.).

9. *Prolegomena*, p. 260.

10. See esp. *Dreams of a Spirit Seer*, p. 370.

11. See, e.g., *Critique*, A127, B165, A216 / B263.

12. Cf. ibid., B127, A609 / B637, A621–2 / B649–50, A635–6 / B663–4.

13. Concerning the Metaphysical/Transcendental Deduction serving as an answer to the second of the three Humean views, cf. *Critique*, B127–8, 168.

14. Ibid., A760–1 / B788–9.

15. AA 2:392, 395–6.

16. The significance of this letter has been best recognized by some of the Francophone literature on Kant, in particular work by H. J. de Vleeschauwer and B. Longuenesse.

17. AA 2:392. Cf. the similar definition of sensibility at *Critique*, A19 / B33.

18. In the letter Kant seems to think that an early version of the *Critique*'s Metaphysical Deduction holds the key to solving this problem. That would turn out not to be quite right in the end, though it did provide the key for solving a closely related problem in which he was about to get interested (Hume's problem concerning the very *existence* of a priori concepts).

19. For Kant's statement of these two problems in the letter to Herz, see *Philosophical Correspondence*, pp. 71–2. Cf. AA 17, nos. 4470, 4473, the former of which approximately sums up these two worries thus: "The primary question is: how concepts of things can arise in us which have not become known to us through any appearance of the things, or propositions which no experience has taught us."

20. I here agree with the scholarly consensus (B. Erdmann, N. Kemp Smith, R. P. Wolff, L. W. Beck, et al.) that Kant was first made aware of Hume's view concerning the causal principle—which is clearly stated only in the *Treatise*, effectively inaccessible to the pre-critical Kant with his poor to non-existent grasp of English because as yet untranslated into German, not in the *Enquiry*, already available to him in German translation since the 1750s—by the 1772 German translation of this work of Beattie's, which contains a clear exposition of the view in question.

21. For example, already in the *Herder Metaphysics* from the early
1760s Kant associates such a position with Aristotle and Locke (AA
28[1]:60; 28[2,1]:851–2, 952 ff.). In subsequent metaphysics lectures
he returns to the subject of this position repeatedly, associating it
mainly with Aristotle (ambiguously), Locke, and Epicurus. Hume was
therefore not the first or even the main figure in whom Kant found
such a position.

22. For example, already in the *Universal Natural History and Theory
of the Heavens* of 1755 Kant had argued that "man . . . has all his concepts and representations from impressions which the universe rouses
in his soul through the body" (AA 1:355). Again, in the *Herder Metaphysics* from the early 1760s he asserts that "all our concepts begin from
sensory feelings," and that all our unanalyzable concepts are sensory
(AA 28[1]:60; 28[2,1]:953). Again, in *Dreams of a Spirit Seer* from 1766
he remarks that "it is, of course, impossible to form any concept of
that which deviates from common empirical concepts and which no
experience can explain, even analogically," and he writes of "empirical
concepts, upon which all our judgments must at all times be based"
(pp. 322, 367–8).

On the other hand, the *Herder Metaphysics* also argues that logical
possibility and impossibility are examples of concepts which are *not*
sensory (AA 28[2,1]:936–8). And similarly, in *Dreams of a Spirit Seer*
Kant qualifies the remarks just quoted to allow for exceptions (p. 320,
footnote). Moreover, exceptions soon afterwards play a major role in
the *Inaugural Dissertation*.

23. For a vacillation between these two worries in a *Reflexion* from
the 1770s, see AA 17, no. 4470.

24. *Critique*, A84 / B116–17. Cf. the discussion of Hume at B127;
also B168.

25. Ibid., A85 / B117.

26. Kant's considered position, not only in the critical writings, but
already in the *Reflexionen* of the 1770s, is that there *are* concepts which
violate the Humean principle (see, e.g., AA 17, nos. 3927, 3930). This
had indeed also been his considered position even earlier, for example
in the *Inaugural Dissertation*.

27. Thus, in the *Critique* Kant would write that "the very concept
of a cause *so manifestly contains the concept of a necessity of connection with
an effect* . . . that the concept would be altogether lost if we attempted
to derive it, as Hume has done, from a repeated association of that
which happens with that which precedes, and from a custom of con-
necting representations, a custom originating in this repeated association, and constituting therefore a merely subjective necessity" (B5, em-

phasis added). Cf. the following remark in the *Mrongovius Metaphysics*
of 1783: "Locke said all concepts are borrowed from experience. Leib-
niz no. We also have some through pure reason. That is easy to decide,
e.g., can experience very well provide the concept of cause and effect
. . . ?" (p. 781).

28. Thus in the *Critique* Kant would write that "the concept of a
cause involves the character of necessity, which no experience can
yield" (A112; cf. A91 / B123–4).

Note that this *confirmed* rather than overturning Kant's predomi-
nant pre-existing intuitions concerning the matter. Already in the
Herder Metaphysics from the early 1760s, for example, he had noted:
"Cognition of [cause and effect] is merely a judgment. I do not see that
lightning sets a house on fire" (AA 28[2,1]:928). And in the *Inaugural
Dissertation* he had argued, similarly, that the concept of a cause was
not derivable from sensation (AA 2:395).

29. Thus in a passage of the *Von Schön Metaphysics* from the critical
period Kant characterizes such a priori concepts as, unlike such a priori
concepts as God, those "to which an object in our experience corresponds," those which "have . . . objective reality, they can be measured
off from the object of experience," those "which we really need in
order to understand the objects which present themselves" (AA
28[1]:470; cf. *Critique*, A720–1 / B748–9).

30. Thus in the *Mrongovius Metaphysics* Kant treats quite respect-
fully a position—which he finds Aristotle and Locke embracing incon-
sistently, but praises Epicurus for embracing consistently—that "if all
concepts are borrowed from experience, then they can accept nothing
except what rests on experience. But God is in no experience. Therefore we cannot say anything about him" (p. 763).

31. Hume, *Enquiry*, sec. 4, pt. 1.

32. Ibid., sec. 12, pt. 3.

33. For reasons which have been pointed out by L. W. Beck and
which are discussed in the next note, it can be questioned whether
this gives a completely accurate account of Hume's view of the causal
principle in the *Treatise*. It does, however, give an accurate account of
Hume's *considered* view of the causal principle as distilled from the
Treatise and the *Enquiry* together. And, more importantly for our present purposes, it gives an accurate account of the view of the causal
principle which Kant—aware of the *Treatise*'s general conclusion concerning the causal principle, but drawing his understanding of the
"fork" which drove Hume to that conclusion rather from the *Enquiry*—would inevitably have *taken* to be Hume's.

34. My implication here that Kant identified Hume's relations of ideas with his own analytic judgments, understanding truth in virtue of the law of contradiction to be definitive of both, is conventional wisdom. It has, however, been challenged by L. W. Beck, at *Essays on Kant and Hume*, pp. 82 ff. Beck argues that, although if one goes by the opening passages of *Enquiry*, sec. 4, where Hume explains relations of ideas, "relations of ideas . . . seem to be judged in what Kant calls analytic judgments," nevertheless "Kant was correct in not taking this to mean that relations of ideas . . . are equivalent to the relation expressed in an analytical judgment." As far as I can see, Beck's only evidence for his implication here that Kant did *not* believe relations of ideas and analytic judgments to be equivalent is the fact that Kant does not explicitly cite the opening paragraphs of *Enquiry*, sec. 4 and point out the equivalence. However, that is very weak evidence indeed. And it seems still weaker when one remembers that, as Beck himself correctly notes, "again and again Kant writes as if Hume had distinguished between analytic and synthetic judgments and had categorically denied the possibility of a priori synthetic judgments." For if Kant did not see relations of ideas—to all appearances defined at *Enquiry*, sec. 4, pt. 1 as principles whose negations violate the law of contradiction, just as Kant defines analytic judgments at *Critique*, B12, 15–16, A151 / B190–1, *Prolegomena*, p. 267, and elsewhere—as Hume's version of analytic judgments, then what *did* Kant see as Hume's version of analytic judgments?! Beck has been misled into his implausible implication that Kant did not regard Humean relations of ideas and his own analytic judgments as equivalent through a more plausible thesis that *if* Kant had read Hume's *Treatise* then he *would* have had reason to distinguish them. Thus Beck writes: "The relations of ideas in the *Enquiry* correspond to the 'necessary and unalterable' philosophical relations of the *Treatise*. But the necessary and unalterable relations are not analytical in the sense that . . . the denial of such a relation involves a contradiction. By 'contradiction' Hume does not mean merely an assertion like 'A is not A.' He means also 'A is not B' where an A that is not a B is 'inconceivable' or 'unimaginable' . . . [Hume's] relations of ideas are not . . . analytic propositions as Kant understood the term, though this cannot be seen by anyone who, like Kant, reads only the *Enquiry* and not also the *Treatise*. Had Kant read Hume's *Treatise*, he would have found Hume tacitly admitting a class of . . . relations of ideas which are not testable by the logical law of contradiction." This more plausible thesis of Beck's still strikes me as inaccurate. Is the situation not rather that the *Enquiry* really does understand its relations of ideas to be based on the law of contradiction in the same way as Kant's analytic

judgments and that this marks a *change of position* from the *Treatise*'s account of its—consequently, only approximately equivalent—necessary and unalterable relations? However, the more important point to note here is that, that question aside, inferring from this more plausible thesis to the conclusion that Kant really did understand Humean relations of ideas and his own analytic judgments to be non-equivalent is a non sequitur. Moreover, it is a non sequitur the implausibility of whose conclusion is sufficiently shown by two facts which Beck acknowledges in his very statement of his more plausible thesis: (1) Kant had *not* read the *Treatise* and (2) the *Enquiry*, which he *had* read, gives no indication that Hume takes as his criterion of relations of ideas anything other than the violation of the law of contradiction by their negations. On the question of whether Kant regarded relations of ideas and analytic judgments as equivalent, then, conventional wisdom proves for once to be wisdom.

35. For example, in the *Prolegomena* he states that "all analytic judgments depend wholly on the principle of contradiction, and are in their nature a priori cognitions" (p. 267). I say "of course" not only because of the intrinsic force of the point, but also because Kant really *already* believed principles true in virtue of the law of contradiction to be knowable a priori, as can be seen, for example, from a passage on causal knowledge at *Dreams of a Spirit Seer*, p. 370.

36. *Critique*, B19. That Hume's "fork," as illustrated in his treatment of the causal principle, did in this way lead Kant to this central puzzle of the critical philosophy is reflected in the fact that the *Critique*, after its first formulation of the puzzle, immediately goes on to say: "Among philosophers, David Hume came nearest to envisaging this problem . . . He occupied himself . . . with the synthetic proposition regarding the connection of an effect with its cause (*principium causalitatis*) and he believed himself to have shown that such an a priori proposition is entirely impossible. If we accept his conclusions, then all that we call metaphysics is a mere delusion" (B19–20).

37. In a passage from his 1794–5 lectures on metaphysics, Kant reportedly went as far as to say the following: "Metaphysics contributes nothing to the extension of empirical principles, to the science of empirical physics: the cognition is quite unnecessary in connection with physics, in that the principles of metaphysics are quite set aside and recognized appearances are the basis, and the fundamental principles derived from them are sufficient for explaining everything. Experience confirms, e.g., the rational propositions: in all changes substance never vanishes but only the form of things, or: each change has its cause; so much so that one simply accepts them without investigating their basis,

and one already becomes certain through experience of their truth under all circumstances" (AA 29[1,2]:947–8).

38. Hence, in a passage from the *Dohna Metaphysics* of 1792–3 Kant gives the causal principle as his paradigmatic example of a priority in a synthetic principle outside of mathematics: "The situation with physical axioms is similar [to that with mathematical propositions]; we know them, are *convinced* of them, without recourse to experience, e.g., all effects have a cause" (AA 28[2,1]:620). And in the *Critique* he gives as a reason for the unacceptability of Hume's account of the causal principle the circumstance that "the concept of a cause *so manifestly* contains the concept . . . of the strict universality [and consequently— since Kant takes strict universality to be a "criterion," i.e., at least a sufficient condition, of a priority; see *Critique*, B3–4—the a priority] of the rule ['every alteration must have a cause']" (B4–5, emphasis added). Cf. *Prolegomena*, p. 275, where Kant argues that we can take it as given that we have synthetic a priori knowledge of the principles of pure physics, which include the causal principle.

39. The causal principle was not, though, for Kant, the only, or even the most compelling, example of synthetic a priori knowledge that could be appealed to in this way in order to refute the now-refined objection; mathematics afforded examples of at least equal force. An analogous point applies in connection with the objections concerning concepts: in Kant's view, mathematics contains clear examples of a priori concepts which both genuinely exist and refer.

40. *Prolegomena*, pp. 258–60.

41. AA 12:371.

42. *Critique*, A50: "When [concepts] contain sensation . . . they are empirical. When there is no mingling of sensation with the representation, they are pure." Cf. AA 17, no. 3965: "A concept which cannot be regarded as an impression of the senses is pure." The slightly broader definition of a concept's "a priority" which I give here in the main text follows from these definitions of a concept's "purity" together with Kant's standard explanation of the distinction between "purity" and "a priority" at *Critique*, B3. Kant does not himself usually distinguish between pure concepts and merely a priori concepts. But he does sometimes imply such a distinction—e.g., at *Critique*, A95 he refers to "pure a priori concepts," and evidently does not intend this expression to be merely pleonastic. The concepts of the understanding in their *purely logical* meanings certainly count as pure concepts. However, in their *schematized* meanings—when, for example, the category of reality gets schematized in terms of *sensation*—they may only be a priori concepts.

43. For Kant's sensitivity to such a possibility, and perception of the need to address it, see for example *Prize Essay*, p. 263, where he interprets the more extreme forms of skepticism which have called into question "even . . . principles of the cognition of the sensible and . . . experience itself" as "perhaps a challenge to the dogmatists . . . to prove those a priori principles on which rests even the possibility of experience, and since they could not do so, to depict experience as doubtful to them as well" (the anacoluthon here is Kant's own).

<h2 style="text-align:center">Chapter Six
Kant's Reformed Metaphysics</h2>

1. *Prolegomena*, p. 371; cf. pp. 255–7, 271–5, 327, 365–71, 383; and *Critique*, A849–51 / B877–9. This fundamental assumption of Kant's is somewhat obscured by the many passages in which he makes less standard uses of the term "metaphysics," and has consequently not always been recognized by the secondary literature. For example, De Vleeschauwer evidently overlooks it when he argues that the critical philosophy saves a metaphysics concerning the subject matter of traditional special metaphysics—"Wie ich jetzt die *Kritik der reinen Vernunft* entwicklungsgeschichtlich lese," p. 363.

2. "Metaphysics actually exists, if not as a science, yet as a natural disposition," which "considered by itself alone . . . is dialectical and illusory" (*Critique*, B21; *Prolegomena*, p. 365).

3. "The term 'metaphysics,' in its *strict* sense, is commonly reserved for the metaphysics of speculative reason [i.e., for theoretical metaphysics—M.N.F.]" (*Critique*, A842 / B870; cf. *Prolegomena*, pp. 278–9; *Prize Essay*, p. 261).

4. There are a few passages in the *Critique* which are potentially very misleading in this connection. At A334–5 / B391–2, and again in a footnote at B395, Kant seems to envisage metaphysics as a science of precisely such items. However, he is here using the word *science* either in an inverted-commas sense or in the sense of a genuine science but one that treats the illusions which occur in connection with such items—cf. A408 / B435: "pretended science"; A841 / B869: metaphysics is "the science which exhibits in systematic connection the whole body (true *as well as illusory*) of philosophical cognition arising out of pure reason" (emphasis added). Again, at A845–7 / B873–5 he gives a very broad definition of metaphysics which includes cognition of such items. However, this definition is immediately preceded by the passage

just quoted from A841 / B869 in which he conceives the discipline as one which contains "true *as well as illusory*" cognition.

5. See ibid., B395, note a. Kant also makes this point repeatedly in the lectures on metaphysics—see, e.g., AA 28(1):301–2, 381–3; 28(2,1):618–20, 774–5, 821–2; 29(1,2):947–8.

6. *Critique*, Bxix. Cf. A471 / B499, A701–2 / B729–30. Also *Prize Essay*, pp. 260, 296–301, 316–17.

7. *Critique*, A50 / B74: "Neither concepts without an intuition in some way corresponding to them nor intuitions without concepts can yield a cognition"; "Thoughts without content are empty, intuitions without concepts are blind."

8. This is obvious enough where *empirical* knowledge is concerned. But according to Kant it is also true of mathematical synthetic a priori knowledge, whose basis in pure intuition requires confirmation by sensible intuitions if it is to constitute real knowledge, and of such *non*-supersensuous metaphysical synthetic a priori knowledge as knowledge of the causal principle, which, although lacking any proof in pure intuition, and although not *derived* from sensible intuitions, nonetheless requires confirmation by sensible intuitions in order to constitute real knowledge. See esp. *Critique*, B147, A156–8 / B195–7; cf. A239–40 / B298–9.

9. Concerning this deeper reason, see esp. *Prize Essay*, pp. 273–7, 296. For Kant this deeper reason (supersensuous metaphysics' lack of the required foundation in intuitions) in effect *explains* the former one (its incurable vulnerability to equipollence problems).

10. *Critique*, Bxix–xxii, Bxxx–xxxi, A470–1 / B498–9, A634 / B662.

11. See ibid., A508 / B536 ff., A616–20 / B644–8, A642–702 / B670–730.

12. See ibid., Axx–xxi, Bxliii, A841 / B869, A845–7 / B873–5. Note that "physiology" here does not imply a restriction to the physical but instead bears the broad etymological sense of a science of nature (*physis*).

13. Cf. *Metaphysical Foundations of Natural Science*, AA 4:469–70, where Kant provides a fuller account than in the *Critique* of how the foundation of the "metaphysics of nature" treated in the Transcendental Analytic relates to the rest of the discipline which it supports.

14. Hence, for example, the *Prolegomena* describes both the causal principle and the principle of the permanence of substance as "metaphysical" (pp. 273, 378). Cf. *Von Schön Metaphysics*, p. 468: "Nature is the object of all possible experience. Here again I can have principles which are not borrowed from experience and these belong to metaphysics, e.g., that all changes have their cause."

15. This helps to explain why Kant announces at *Critique*, A247 / B303 that "the . . . name of an Ontology [i.e., general ontology—M.N.F.] . . . must give place to the . . . title of an . . . Analytic of the pure understanding [i.e., Kant's metaphysics of nature—M.N.F.]."

It is interesting to note that Kant's project of reducing metaphysics to general ontology (or something like it) had some earlier precedents in Germany, for example in Stahl (see Wundt, *Die deutsche Schulmetaphysik des 17. Jahrhunderts*, pp. 171, 219–20, 223–7).

16. This motive behind Kant's conception of the discipline is visible, for example, in a passage from the *Von Schön Metaphysics* where, after distinguishing between two types of a priori concept, those to which an object corresponds in experience and those to which it does not, Kant observes: "The aggregate of these pure concepts of the understanding to which an object in experience does correspond constitutes transcendental philosophy or ontology [i.e., metaphysics of nature—M.N.F.]" (p. 470).

17. Concerning a priority serving as a distinctive mark of metaphysics for the critical philosophy, see, e.g., *Prolegomena*, pp. 265–6. Concerning supersensuousness having done so for traditional metaphysics, and also concerning the distinction between a priority and supersensuousness, see esp. *Prize Essay*, pp. 316–19.

18. It deserves emphasis, because the point is commonly overlooked, that the term "a priori" means very different things for Kant depending on whether he is applying it to concepts or to principles. For one thing, when applied to concepts it signifies a certain sort of independence from *sensations*, whereas when applied to principles it signifies a certain sort of independence from *experience* (where experience is far from being the same as sensation).

19. Some textual evidence for this was presented in an earlier note (ch. 5, n. 42).

20. *Mrongovius Metaphysics*, p. 762: "All concepts of the understanding would mean nothing if the senses did not supply any objects and examples. If I, for example, explained as much as you like what a substance was, but did not know how to give any example, then all would be in vain . . . But it is quite true that the concepts of the understanding are not borrowed from the senses."

21. *Prize Essay*, p. 317: "We . . . can distinguish the cognition a priori . . . which, though grounded a priori, can nevertheless find the objects for its concepts in experience, from that . . . whose object . . . lies beyond all bounds of experience." Cf. p. 260: in considering that super*sensuousness* knowledge of which has traditionally been metaphysics' goal, "We count as sensuous, though, not only that whose repre-

sentation is considered in relation to the senses, but also in relation to the understanding, just so long as the understanding's pure concepts are thought of in their application to objects of the senses, and hence for the purpose of a possible *experience*." Also p. 319, where Kant accuses traditional metaphysics of failing to mark this distinction between different types of a priori concepts. Also, *Von Schön Metaphysics*, p. 470.

22. *Von Schön Metaphysics*, p. 470: "The aggregate of these pure concepts of the understanding to which an object in experience does correspond constitutes transcendental philosophy or ontology [i.e., metaphysics of nature—M.N.F.]."

23. *Critique*, B2–3.

24. *Mrongovius Metaphysics*, p. 768: "There are two sorts of uses of the pure understanding: the immanent is namely that in which a priori cognitions have their objects in experience. In just the same way there are also a priori axioms which concern objects of experience—that is pure reason, but in its immanent use . . . And there is the transcendent use, namely that in which a priori cognitions do not have their objects in experience." Cf. *Prize Essay*, pp. 317–19, where Kant again draws this distinction, and accuses traditional metaphysics of failing to mark it. At *Critique*, A764–5 / B792–3 Kant takes *Hume* to task for failing to mark the distinction as well: "We suppose ourselves to be able to pass a priori beyond our concept, and so to extend our cognition. This we attempt to do either through the pure understanding, in respect of that which is at least capable of being an *object of experience*, or through pure reason, in respect of such properties of things as can never be met with in experience. [Hume] did not distinguish these two kinds of judgments, as he yet ought to have done, but straightway proceeded to treat this self-increment of concepts, and, as we may say, this spontaneous generation on the part of our understanding and of our reason, without impregnation by experience, as being impossible."

25. See *Critique*, B3–5.

26. Kant points out at *Critique*, A184–5 / B228 that he was the first to notice that the synthetic a priori principles involved "are valid only in relation to possible experience, and can therefore be proved . . . through a deduction of the possibility of experience."

27. Thus Kant writes that "its principles are merely rules for the exposition of *appearances*; and the proud name of an Ontology that presumptuously claims to supply . . . synthetic a priori cognitions of things in general [i.e., things in themselves—M.N.F.] . . . must, therefore, give place to the modest title of a mere Analytic of pure understanding" (ibid., A247 / B303).

28. Concerning this, see esp. *Critique*, A832–51 / B860–79; *Von Schön Metaphysics*, pp. 463–5; *Prize Essay*, p. 321.

29. See esp. *Critique*, A726–37 / B754–65. Kant's early rejection of this mathematical model as unsuited to metaphysics is most conspicuous in his *Inquiry concerning the Distinctness of the Principles of Natural Theology and Morality* from 1764.

30. Only "roughly" due to a modest exception which Kant explains at *Critique*, A71–2 / B97 concerning "infinite" judgments.

31. Note that Kant extends such systematicity beyond his "metaphysics of nature" as well, envisaging in addition a systematicity among the three transcendent ideas of the world as a whole, the soul, and God established by their one-to-one correlation with the three traditional forms of syllogism (see *Critique*, A333–8 / B390–6; *Prolegomena*, p. 330).

32. See *Critique*, Bxix, A841 / B869, A849–51 / B877–9. Cf. AA 17:259, 261, 495–6, 552–3, 558, 613.

33. *Critique*, A841–2 / B869–70. Cf. *Prolegomena*, p. 279, where Kant *distinguishes* from metaphysics this "transcendental philosophy"—an expression which he here uses in this sense (as, e.g., at *Critique*, A65–6 / B90–1), not, as often elsewhere, in the sense of metaphysics of nature (e.g., at *Critique*, A13–15 / B27–9; AA 29[1,2]:949, 970). Also, a 1783 letter to Garve in which Kant writes that "it is not at all metaphysics that the *Critique* is doing but a whole new science, never before attempted, namely, the critique of an a priori judging reason" (*Philosophical Correspondence*, p. 102). Also, *Philosophical Encyclopedia*, at AA 29(1,1):11–12.

CHAPTER SEVEN

DEFENSES AGAINST HUMEAN SKEPTICISM

1. See *Critique*, B19–20; *Prolegomena*, pp. 272–3.

2. Thus in connection with the puzzle of how a priori concepts can refer, Kant draws a distinction between two sides of the section of the *Critique* which addresses the puzzle, the Transcendental Deduction, implying that one side *proves that* the a priori concepts treated there refer, while the other side *explains the possibility* of their being employed by us to refer: "The one [side] . . . is intended to expound . . . the objective validity of [the pure understanding's] a priori concepts . . . The other [side] seeks to investigate the pure understanding itself, its possibility . . . and so deals with it in its subjective aspect" (*Critique*, Axvi–

xvii). Recognizing Kant's dual strategy is therefore essential for properly understanding this famous distinction between an "objective" and
a "subjective" side of the Transcendental Deduction (though it should
be noted that he here runs together with the distinction between these
two strategies certain further distinctions).

Similarly, in relation to the puzzle of synthetic a priori knowledge,
Kant promises both an explanation of the possibility of such knowledge and a proof of the truth of particular cases of it: the *Critique*
"enables us to explain how there can be cognition a priori; and in addition, to furnish satisfactory proofs of the laws which form the a priori
basis of nature" (*Critique*, Bxix).

Kant's distinction at *Prolegomena*, pp. 274–6 between the partly
"synthetical" method of the *Critique* and the exclusively "analytical"
method of the *Prolegomena* is again in large part a distinction between
the *proving that* and the *explaining the possibility* sides of his strategy
respectively. Thus he says there that the analytical method, in contrast
to the synthetical, does not answer the question "*whether* [synthetic a
priori cognition] is possible . . . but *how* it is possible" (p. 275; cf.
p. 276).
3. By contrast, the corresponding material in the *Prolegomena* develops only the "analytical," or *explaining the possibility*, side of the strategy,
due to the work's more popular function (see pp. 274–5).

Again by contrast, but this time for more principled reasons, in the
Transcendental Aesthetic of the *Critique*, the a priori intuitions/con-
cepts of space and time and the a priori concepts and synthetic a priori
principles of mathematics are considered by Kant to be so secure that
they can (and probably also must) dispense with any special proof of
reference or truth, and instead receive only an explanation of their
possibility as cognition (see *Critique*, A149 / B188–9, A261 / B316–17,
A732–3 / B760–1). The main reason for this asymmetry to the advan-
tage of mathematics over metaphysics lies, according to Kant, in the
role of *a priori intuition* as a sphere for expounding and guaranteeing
the validity of the former but not of the latter (see, e.g., ibid., A87–8 /
B120, A732–3 / B760–1; *Mrongovius Metaphysics*, p. 765).
4. For example, Kant says of the *proving that* or "objective" side of
the Transcendental Deduction's defense of the a priori concepts of
the understanding: "The objective validity of the categories as a priori
concepts rests . . . on the fact that . . . through them alone does experience become possible" (*Critique*, A93 / B126; cf. A217 / B264 on the
Analogies of Experience).
5. Cf. R.C.S. Walker, *Kant* (London: Routledge and Kegan Paul,
1978), p. 10. The particular type of experience involved varies from

argument to argument. For example, in the Transcendental Deduction it is experience simpliciter, in the First Analogy experience of objective succession or co-existence, in the Second Analogy experience of objective events, and in the Third Analogy experience of the co-existence of objects in space.

6. Kant's summary of the argument of the Third Analogy is one of his clearer expressions of this whole model: "Substances must stand . . . in dynamical community if their co-existence is to be cognized in any possible experience. Now, in respect to the objects of experience, everything without which the experience of these objects would not itself be possible is necessary. It is therefore necessary that all substances in the [field of] appearance, so far as they co-exist, should stand in thoroughgoing community of interaction" (*Critique*, A212–13 / B259–60).

7. Much of the voluminous secondary literature on "transcendental arguments" has in mind a significantly different type of argument: one concerned with conditions of the possibility—not of experience, or empirical knowledge but—of *meaning*. This type of argument does not play any central role in Kant. However, as we shall see in chapter 12, something like it does play an implicit role in his views about formal logic.

8. Revealing this motive, Kant says in the *Mrongovius Metaphysics* of 1783, for example: "Must there not be certain synthetic judgments a priori through which the synthetic judgments a posteriori are possible? And they were certainly true because they provide the foundation of experience, and experience is true . . . We will show that [the a priori axioms on which the possibility of experience rests] are certain because experience is certain and experience rests upon them . . . The a priori proposition which precedes all experience is certain, for what is more certain than experience?, and experience is certain only to the extent that the a priori proposition permits" (pp. 794, 799, 805).

9. Transcendental idealism was originally motivated by reflection on, and applied to, the former subject matter (space, time, and mathematics), namely in the *Inaugural Dissertation* of 1770. It was only later extended to cover the latter subject matter as well (the a priori concepts of the understanding and the metaphysical synthetic a priori principles associated with them).

10. Thus, in the *Prolegomena* Kant says that he realized that "they were not derived from experience, as Hume had tried, but sprang from the pure understanding" (p. 260). And in the *Critique* he begins the Transcendental Analytic with a declaration that the task of transcendental philosophy is "to investigate the possibility of concepts a priori

by looking for them in the understanding alone, as their birthplace," to "follow up the pure concepts to their first seeds and dispositions in the human understanding" (A66 / B90–1).

The Metaphysical Deduction's tracing of the twelve a priori concepts of the understanding back to the twelve logical forms of judgment, which immediately follows these remarks in the *Critique*, is meant to *establish* the central thesis of their origin in the understanding. Thus Kant says later in the text: "In the *metaphysical deduction* the a priori origin of the categories has been proved through their complete agreement with the general logical functions of thought" (B159).

Ironically, Kant had already possessed this solution to Hume's problem, in its essentials, *before* he took the problem itself deeply to heart in or shortly after 1772. Thus, the *Inaugural Dissertation* of 1770 already asserts the origin of these concepts in the understanding or intellect, as opposed to sensibility (AA 2:395), and that assertion is in effect repeated by the letter to Herz of 1772, which in addition already sketches an early version of the project of their Metaphysical Deduction (*Philosophical Correspondence*, p. 73). This chronological antecedence of the solution to its problem in Kant's development may seem strange, but is not really so surprising on reflection; one factor which quite often makes a problem come to seem interesting to an inquirer is a sense that he has the resources for solving it.

11. See *Critique*, A243 / B301; cf. *Volckmann Metaphysics*, p. 404. This is Kant's considered solution to Hume's problem concerning the origin of the concept of causal necessity. It should be noted, however, that Kant sometimes muddies these relatively clear waters by also equating causal necessity with the necessity of the causal principle (*Critique*, B4–5, A766–7 / B794–5), or even with the necessity of a particular causal law (A91 / B123–4).

12. *Critique*, A93 / B126: "through them alone does experience become possible." This statement should now be read in a causal or quasi-causal sense, and while keeping in mind Kant's position that "the a priori conditions of a possible experience in general are at the same time conditions of the possibility of objects of experience" (ibid., A111; cf. A158 / B197; also *Dohna Metaphysics*, p. 654).

13. Thus at *Critique*, A92–3 / B124–6 Kant writes: "There are only two possible ways in which synthetic representations and their objects can establish connection, obtain necessary relation to one another, and, as it were, meet one another. Either the object alone must make the representation possible, or the representation alone must make the object possible [i.e., the two possibilities which Kant had already recognized in the letter to Herz—M.N.F.]. In the former case, this

relation is only empirical, and the representation is never possible a priori. This is true of appearances, as regards that in them which belongs to sensation. In the latter case, representation in itself does not produce its object in so far as *existence* is concerned, for we are not here speaking of its causality by means of the will [i.e., as in the case of the sort of divine archetypal intellect envisaged by the letter to Herz— M.N.F.]. Nonetheless, the representation is a priori determinant of the object, if it be the case that only through the representation is it possible to *cognize* anything *as an object* . . . Concepts of objects in general . . . underlie all empirical cognition as its a priori conditions. The objective validity of the categories as a priori concepts rests, therefore, on the fact that, so far as the form of thought is concerned, through them alone does experience become possible. They relate of necessity and a priori to objects of experience, for the reason that only by means of them can any object whatsoever of experience be thought" (cf. A95–7, 128–30; Bxvii–xviii, 166–7). See also *Von Schön Metaphysics*, p. 474: "How can I have a priori concepts of things before they have presented themselves to me? The categories are concerned solely with objects of possible experience and the categories are valid precisely because they contain the conditions under which experience first becomes possible. Consequently, what contains the ground of the possibility of experience also contains the ground of the possibility of the object."

14. Accordingly, Kant writes towards the end of the Transcendental Deduction, as he is about to embark on the Schematism chapter, that "how [the a priori concepts of the understanding] make experience possible . . . will be shown more fully in the following chapter" (*Critique*, B167).

15. See ibid., A137–47 / B176–87, A240–6 / B300–2.

16. See ibid., A144 / B183, A243 / B301.

17. For classic statements of this thesis, see ibid., A113–14, 125–6, Bxvi–xviii. Note that the two motives behind the thesis of transcendental idealism which I have in effect just identified—explaining the reference of a priori concepts and explaining the possibility of synthetic a priori knowledge—are complemented by a third: explaining the *necessity* of synthetic a priori knowledge. This third motive was actually the one that first induced Kant to develop the thesis, namely in the *Inaugural Dissertation* (the other two motives only coming into play later). During the critical period Kant often tends to run this third problem concerning necessity together with the problem of how synthetic a priori knowledge is possible—something that is easy for him to do due to the intimacy of the connection that he sees between necessity and

a priority (see ibid., B3–4). However, it is really a distinct problem—an *ontological* problem in contrast to an epistemological one.

CHAPTER EIGHT
DEFENSES AGAINST PYRRHONIAN SKEPTICISM

1. *Critique*, B19.
2. Ibid., B22.
3. See ibid., A423–4 / B451–2, A740 / B768.
4. I shall here simplify what could easily become a long story in its own right. Kant's strategies for resolving the Antinomies are rather unsettled even within the *Critique*, and that is even truer of the whole history of his attempts to resolve them (including such earlier works as the *Inaugural Dissertation* of 1770 and such later ones as *On a Discovery* of 1790).
5. *Critique*, A506 / B534. In the "Mathematical" Antinomies each side's proof of its principle takes the "apagogical" form of (1) a disproof, by reductio ad absurdum, of the principle asserted on the other side, from which (2) an inference to the truth of the principle to be proved is then drawn in light of the two principles' apparent exhaustion of the logical possibilities. Kant in each case accepts that step (1) is compelling, but (as we are about to see) not that step (2) is.
6. Kant sometimes—for instance, prominently in the *Prolegomena*, and at *Critique*, A740 / B768—develops his diagnosis of these Antinomies in terms of a more specific claim that the concept of the whole spatio-temporal world as it occurs in them is actually self-contradictory.
7. See *Critique*, A502–6 / B530–4, A740 / B768, A792–3 / B820–1; *Prolegomena*, pp. 341–2.
8. See *Critique*, A529–37 / B557–65, A559–65 / B587–93; *Prolegomena*, pp. 343–7.
9. *Critique*, B22–3.
10. Ibid., B22. Cf. A476–81 / B504–9, A761 / B789.
11. Cf. ibid., A761–4 / B789–92, A768–9 / B796–7.
12. Ibid., Axv. Another route to the same interpretive conclusion is to note that because these conditional propositions involve necessity, they must in Kant's eyes be a priori (ibid., B3–4), and that he believes a priori knowledge quite generally to be apodeictically certain: "Everything that is to be cognized a priori is thereby announced as apodeictically certain" (*Prolegomena*, p. 369; cf. *Critique*, A775 / B803, A822–3 / B850–1).

13. Recall *Blomberg Logic*, p. 214: "People . . . blamed Pyrrho for doubting the truth of all empirical judgments and not placing faith in them. However, this is a pure invention which has no basis at all."

14. Recall Kant's implication at ibid., p. 214 that for Pyrrho there are "certain, so to speak, eternal principles of our reason [i.e., *logic* and mathematics—M.N.F.], which cannot be disputed at all."

15. Here again, the fact that Kant clearly understands these explanations to be a priori points to the same interpretive conclusion.

16. *Critique*, Aix.

17. *Prolegomena*, p. 371.

18. Ibid., p. 383. Cf. *Critique*, A12 / B26: transcendental philosophy provides "a touchstone of the value, or lack of value, of all a priori cognition."

19. In Kant's view, once expelled, some of them will in fact go on to win their wars, though by means of *practical* justifications, and with a status short of knowledge, which radically distinguish them from metaphysical principles properly so called (the "postulates" of practical reason). Others, accordingly, will perish (their contraries). And still others will in a sense war on indefinitely, though the critical philosopher, recognizing that such questions are not rationally decidable, will refrain from pursuing them any further (*Volckmann Metaphysics*, p. 379: the critical philosophy leads to "complete rest" in connection with metaphysical disputes, "since our reason ceases to ask questions when she sees that this or that is no object for her").

20. *Critique*, Axx, xiv; emphasis added. Cf. Bxxiii–xxiv, B89–92. Also, *Metaphysical Foundations of Natural Science*, AA 4:473: "In all that is called metaphysics the absolute completeness of the sciences may be hoped for . . . ; and therefore just as in the metaphysics of nature in general, so . . . also the completeness of the metaphysics of corporeal nature may be confidently expected."

21. *Prize Essay*, p. 321: "Metaphysics distinguishes itself quite especially among all sciences by being the only one which can be presented completely fully, so that nothing more remains for posterity to add or [with which] to extend metaphysics in its content, indeed so that if the absolute whole does not emerge systematically from the idea of metaphysics, its idea can be considered as having not been correctly understood." *Prolegomena*, p. 365: "A critique of reason must itself exhibit the whole stock of a priori concepts, their division in accordance with their various sources—sensibility, understanding, and reason—and further, a complete table of them and the analysis of all these concepts together with everything which can be derived from them, and then especially the possibility of synthetic a priori cognition by means

of the deduction of these concepts, the fundamental principles of their use, and finally the bounds of their use, but it must do all this in a complete system."

22. See esp. *Critique*, A832–3 / B860–1. Also A403: "in order to show the systematic interconnection of . . . , and so to show that we have them in their completeness . . ." Kant is especially explicit about this strategy in relation to the a priori concepts of the understanding. For example, at *Critique*, A64–5 / B89 he responds to the challenge of demonstrating their completeness with the following declaration of strategy: "When a science is an aggregate brought into existence in a merely experimental manner, such completeness can never be guaranteed by any kind of mere estimate. It is possible only by means of *an idea of the totality* of the a priori cognition yielded by the understanding; such an idea can furnish an exact classification of the concepts which compose that totality, exhibiting their *interconnection in a system*" (cf. A66–7 / B91–2, A80–1 / B106–7; and esp. *Prolegomena*, p. 322).

Incidentally, Kant's possession of this strategy vis-à-vis the a priori concepts of the understanding has often been overlooked by the secondary literature. For example, Koerner accuses Kant of failing to demonstrate the uniqueness of his categorial schema, and thereby overlooks both the fact that Kant was acutely aware of the need to do so, and the fact that he had this strategy for doing so (S. Koerner, "The Impossibility of Transcendental Deductions," *The Monist*, no. 51 [1967]).

23. To illustrate this point with the help of a homely example, a child might be able to show that he had an entire system of Lego pieces by constructing, say, a toy helicopter from them (like the one pictured on the box), but an inference from that fact to his having a complete collection of all Lego pieces would by no means be trivial; indeed in this case it would be massively mistaken.

24. "In order to know whether a type of cognition is completed one must already have a concept of the whole; and so any science must constitute a system, a whole in accordance with an already discovered idea . . . The whole of our pure cognition a priori or of our pure rational cognition is metaphysics, or it is a system of pure rational cognition from mere concepts . . . There lies in human cognition the wherewithal for a system, a system of pure concepts, i.e., for metaphysics: there is hence a system of pure rational cognition a priori . . . If I use my reason merely a priori through concepts, then experience does not guarantee my cognition, since a mere rational concept tolerates no admixture of experience and so here there is more danger that I go wrong, since no experience supports me. Such a science will often

come upon things which tolerate no application in experience, and so we lose an important touchstone of truth; we can no longer test our judgment by experience and it is easy to see that consequently the use of pure reason becomes very slippery [i.e., the equipollence problem— – M.N.F.]. Given this danger which pure reason constantly runs of going astray, we see very easily that it is necessary to examine in advance (1) whether there really is, then, such a pure rational faculty [i.e., it is necessary to explain how such concepts can refer and such principles constitute knowledge—M.N.F.], (2) whether this reason provides us with any genuine cognition [i.e., it is necessary to prove that specific such concepts refer and specific such principles are true—M.N.F.], and (3) whether we can determine the scope and boundaries of pure reason . . . Without an ability to determine whether pure reason can judge, without knowing its boundaries and scope, nothing protects us from error; we in that case fall into illusions and chimeras without recognizing them as such. And that is precisely why people could challenge all its propositions [i.e., the equipollence problem—M.N.F.] before there was a critique of reason" (*Von Schön Metaphysics*, pp. 463–5).

25. *Critique*, A832 / B860: "By an architectonic I understand the art of constructing systems."

26. Kant certainly also has additional motives for wanting to demonstrate the entire systematicity of his new metaphysics besides the one under discussion here. For example, Lambert had argued that the consistency and harmony characteristic of an entire system made it a criterion of truth (see Beck, *Early German Philosophy*, p. 407). And there is a strong element of such a position in Kant as well. Thus, we find him arguing in the *Prize Essay* of 1791 that "when a system is so constituted that, *first*, each principle in it is independently provable, and *second*, if one had any concern about its correctness, still even as a mere hypothesis it leads inevitably to all the remaining principles of the system as consequences, then nothing more can be required in order to recognize its truth" (p. 311; it is of course the second point that is pertinent here; cf. *Critique*, A65 / B90, A647 / B675; also, Kant's lectures on metaphysics, which in places almost sound as though they are advancing a coherence theory of truth; also, Kant's remark in his 1799 open letter on Fichte's *Wissenschaftslehre* that so far from having meant the *Critique* to be only a propaedeutic rather than "the actual system of [transcendental] philosophy . . . I took the completeness of pure philosophy within the *Critique of Pure Reason* to be the best indication of the truth of my work" [*Philosophical Correspondence*, p. 254]). Again— though largely because of the two motives already mentioned—Kant stipulates that entire systematicity is required for *scientificness*: "system-

atic unity is what first raises ordinary cognition to the rank of science" (*Critique*, A832 / B860; cf. *Von Schön Metaphysics*, p. 463: "A system of a type of cognition is called a science . . . In order to know whether a type of cognition is complete one must already have a concept of the whole; and so any science must constitute a system").

27. *Critique*, A64–81 / B89–107; *Prolegomena*, pp. 322–6; *Prize Essay*, pp. 271–2; *Volckmann Metaphysics*, p. 400.

28. *Critique*, A148 / B187, A161 / B200. Kant gives a helpful tabular summary of all these correspondences at *Prolegomena*, pp. 302–3.

29. *Critique*, A243 / B301. Cf. *Volckmann Metaphysics*, p. 404.

30. *Critique*, Bxiv.

CHAPTER NINE
SOME RELATIVELY EASY PROBLEMS

1. "The proud name of an Ontology [i.e., general ontology—M.N.F.] . . . must . . . give place to the modest title of a mere Analytic of the pure understanding [i.e., Kant's metaphysics of nature—M.N.F.]" (*Critique*, A247 / B303). In the *Prize Essay* Kant simply *calls* it ontology: "Ontology is that science (as part of metaphysics) which is constituted by a system of all concepts and fundamental principles of the understanding, but only so far as they refer to objects which can be given to the senses, and can therefore be validated by experience" (p. 260). He generally does so in the lectures on metaphysics as well.

2. Strictly speaking, one should say here, more cautiously, "the *apparent* etymologically derived force." For it is not clear that the word bore this sense in its original application to Aristotle's work, rather than, more mundanely, "after the *Physics*" (i.e., after the latter work of Aristotle's in some cataloguing scheme). In the lectures on metaphysics, Kant shows that he is fully aware of this alternative way of interpreting the expression, but consistently rejects it in favor of the interpretation assumed here (AA 29[1]:174, 381–2, 468; 28[2,1]:616; 29[1,2]:773, 947).

3. Kant makes this point at *Prize Essay*, pp. 315–16.

4. Hence, for example, we read in the *Prolegomena*: "As concerns the sources of metaphysical cognition, its very concept implies that they cannot be empirical. Its principles (including not only its basic propositions but also its basic concepts) must never be derived from experience. It must not be physical but metaphysical knowledge, i.e., knowledge lying beyond experience. It can therefore have for its basis

neither external experience, . . . nor internal . . . It is therefore *a priori* cognition" (pp. 265–6).

5. "No one attempts to establish a science unless he has an idea upon which to base it. But in the working out of the science the schema, nay even the definition, which, at the start, he first gave of the science, is very seldom adequate to his idea. For this idea lies hidden in reason, like a germ in which the parts are still undeveloped and barely recognisable . . . Consequently, . . . we must not explain and determine [sciences] according to the description which their founder gives of them, but in conformity with the idea which, out of the natural unity of the parts that we have assembled, we find to be grounded in reason itself. For we shall then find that its founder, and often even his latest successors, are groping for an idea which they have never succeeded in making clear to themselves, and that consequently they have not been in a position to determine the proper content, the articulation . . . , and limits of the science" (*Critique*, A834 / B862; cf. *Prize Essay*, p. 342, where Kant applies this model to metaphysics specifically).

6. Consider especially T. S. Kuhn's observations on the role of "paradigm shifts" in the development of sciences in his important and influential book *The Structure of Scientific Revolutions* (Chicago: The University of Chicago Press, 1970).

<h2 style="text-align:center">CHAPTER TEN
A METAPHYSICS OF MORALS?</h2>

1. *Critique*, Bxliii, A841–2 / B869–70, A850 / B878.

2. Ibid., A842 / B870; cf. *Prolegomena*, pp. 278–9.

3. See *Critique*, A14–15 / B28–9, A54–5 / B79. I say that this is questionable because it is difficult to see why empirical concepts would have to be any more essentially or deeply involved in the "metaphysics of morals" as Kant officially conceives it than in his "metaphysics of nature."

4. See, for example, ibid., Bxiv, Bxxx, A744–5 / B772–3, A805 / B833, A828–9 / B856–7; *Prolegomena*, pp. 278–9, 371.

5. For example, we read at *Critique*, A14 / B28 that "the highest principles and fundamental concepts of morality are a priori *Erkenntnisse*," and at Bxxi that "when all progress in the field of the supersensible has . . . been denied to speculative reason, it is still open to us to inquire whether, in the practical *Erkenntnis* of reason, data may not

be found sufficient to determine reason's transcendent concept of the unconditioned, and so enable us . . . , though only from a practical point of view, to pass beyond the limits of all possible experience." Cf. A633–4 / B661–2. Also, *Prize Essay*, pp. 281, 310.

6. See *Critique*, Bxix–xxii, Bxxx–xxxi, A744–5 / B772–3, A823 / B851, A828 / B856. Cf. *Pölitz Metaphysics*, AA 28(1):304.

7. For example, in the important passages at *Critique*, A50 / B74 where Kant presents his fundamental principle that all knowledge requires both concepts and intuitions, the word that he uses for knowledge is throughout *Erkenntnis*. (There is therefore *some* ground for N. Kemp Smith's usual practice of translating both words as *knowledge*. However, this conflation of the two words is for the most part extremely confusing, and has therefore been avoided in the present essay, where only *Wissen* has been translated as *knowledge*, but *Erkenntnis* instead as *cognition*.)

8. Kant's clearest account of this generic sense of the word *Erkenntnis* occurs at *Critique of Judgment*, AA 5:467 ff., where he explains that "*Erkennbare* things are threefold in kind: things of opinion (opinabile), things of fact (scibile) [i.e., knowable, *scio* being Latin for *to know*—M.N.F.], and things of faith [*Glaubenssachen*] (mere credibile)."

Kant also uses the word *Erkenntnis* in certain further senses which are less relevant here. For example, in one of its senses it is not restricted to judgments at all, but also includes such truth-valueless items as concepts and intuitions (see, e.g., *Critique*, A320 / B376–7).

9. *Logic*, AA 9:70; cf. *Critique*, A822 / B850.

10. *Logic*, p. 66; cf. *Critique*, A820 / B848, A822 / B850.

11. *Logic*, p. 66; cf. *Critique*, A822 / B850. Two further points to note: (1) Kant also says that whereas *Wissen* is certain, *Glaube* is uncertain—but since he does not seem to stick to the latter half of this position consistently, I shall bracket it here. (2) He distinguishes *Glaube* from mere *Meinung*, which is both objectively and subjectively insufficient.

12. "Even after reason has failed in all its ambitious attempts to pass beyond the limits of all experience, there is still enough left to satisfy us, so far as our practical standpoint is concerned. No one, indeed, will be able to boast that he *knows* [*wisse*] that there is a God, and a future life; if he knows this, he is the very man for whom I have long [and vainly] sought. All knowledge [*Wissen*], if it concerns an object of mere reason, can be communicated; and I might therefore hope that under his instruction my own knowledge would be extended in this wonderful fashion. No, my conviction is not *logical*, but *moral* certainty; and since it rests on subjective grounds (of the moral sentiment), I must not even say, '*It is* morally certain that there is a God, etc.' but '*I am*

morally certain, etc.' In other words, belief in a God and in another world is so interwoven with my moral sentiment that as there is little danger of my losing the latter, there is equally little cause for fear that the former can ever be taken from me" (*Critique*, A828–9 / B856–7; note that moral sentiment had played a fundamental role in Kant's moral theory in *Dreams of a Spirit Seer*, and that it still plays a significant, though far more qualified, role in the *Metaphysics of Morals* of 1797). Cf. *Pölitz Metaphysics*, p. 304.

13. See *Dreams of a Spirit Seer*, pp. 372–3.

14. See *Critique*, Bxxviii, B29, A548 / B576, A800–2 / B828–30, A807 / B835, A841 / B869; *Groundwork of the Metaphysics of Morals* (1785), at AA 4:442–3; *Metaphysics of Morals* (1797), at AA 6:375–7. Kant had indeed already officially taken this step from a sentimentalist to a cognitivist theory in the *Inaugural Dissertation* of 1770, at AA 2:396.

15. Thus at *Critique*, A54–5 / B79 Kant represents pure morals as analogous to general logic. The analogy lies mainly in the facts that (1) the categorical imperative is an a priori principle which is valid for all reason as such, not merely for all human reason (see *Groundwork of the Metaphysics of Morals*, pp. 411–12), i.e., just like general logic, and (2) the categorical imperative appeals to the criterion of avoiding contradiction (in a maxim under universalization), i.e., just as the logical law of contradiction does.

The analogy does have certain limits in Kant's view, in particular because he conceives the categorical imperative to be *synthetic* a priori, like *transcendental* rather than general logic (see ibid., p. 420). However, these are not limits that make it any less cognitive in nature.

16. It is true that Kant is reluctant to say that logical insight itself is either objective or a matter of *Wissen*: "General logic . . . abstracts from all content of cognition, that is, from any reference of it to the object, and treats only the logical form in the relation of any bit of cognition to another" (*Critique*, B79). However, he could hardly appeal to this fact in order to support his position at *Critique*, A828–9 / B856–7. For there is a world of difference between denying that morality is *Wissen* because it is merely a matter of sentiment and doing so because it is like logic—roughly, the difference between saying that it is *less than Wissen* and saying that it is *more than Wissen*. Accordingly, if he were to appeal to this fact in order to justify denying that morality, and hence whatever else rests upon it, is *Wissen*, and therefore excluding them from metaphysics "in its strict sense," the appropriate response would be that this fact would not show morality, and hence whatever else rests upon it, to fall short of metaphysics "in its strict

sense," but instead to be metaphysics in an *even stricter* sense than mere *Wissen* can be.

17. Perhaps because of this problem, Kant elsewhere at about this time seems to cast around for alternative ways of justifying his denial to morality—and hence to whatever else is based upon it as well—of the status of genuine *Wissen(schaft)*. But without greater success. For instance, in the *Mrongovius Metaphysics* of 1783 he writes concerning moral principles: "Not every natural use of reason can be turned into a scientific [*wissenschaftlichen*] one . . . For example, in morality one cannot represent the rule *in abstracto*, but merely *in concreto*. It is, for example, hardly possible to *prove* a priori or to show *in abstracto* the impermissibility of lies; *in concreto* it can indeed be done" (p. 782). His idea here seems to be that since the categorical imperative is a principle for testing *individual* maxims (or intentions), it can only show the moral impermissibility of *general classes* of maxims via showing the moral impermissibility of individual ones (e.g., it can only show the moral impermissibility of intending to lie in general via showing the moral impermissibility of my intending to lie to Mary in order to prevent her from disliking me, the moral impermissibility of Smith's intending to lie to Jones in order to avoid paying him, and so on). However, it is unclear why Kant thinks that such a characteristic of cognition should disqualify it from counting as *Wissen(schaft)*. Moreover, claiming that it did so would carry some very awkward consequences for him, such as, for example, that empirically established laws of nature cannot count as *Wissen(schaft)* either (since they too are established, not directly, but via particular instances). So here again he seems in the end to be left without any good rationale for denying that morality—and hence whatever else is based upon it as well—is *Wissen(schaft)*, and so for denying that it belongs to metaphysics "in its strict sense."

18. In the *Groundwork of the Metaphysics of Morals* the word *Erkenntnis* predominates throughout. There is one reference to moral *Wissen* (p. 457), but it is ambiguous, and in effect soon taken back (p. 462). There are also a couple of references to a *Wissenschaft* of morals (pp. 388, 405), but they are not prominent or emphatic.

19. There is an exception at *Critique of Practical Reason*, p. 91, where the word *Wissenschaft* is used, but the text goes on to back away from this, implying that instead only a *love* of science is involved (pp. 108–9; cf. 150–1).

20. Ibid., p. 163.

21. Ibid., p. 4: "Freedom is . . . the only one of the ideas of speculative reason of which we *know* [*wissen*] the possibility a priori, without

though understanding it, because it is the condition of the moral law, which we know [*wissen*]."

22. *Critique of Judgment*, p. 468: "And, what is very remarkable, there is one rational idea . . . which also comes under things of fact. This is the idea of *freedom*, whose reality . . . may be exhibited by means of practical laws of pure reason, and conformably to this, in actual actions . . . This is the only one of all the ideas of pure reason whose object is a thing of fact and to be reckoned under the *scibilia*."

23. Ibid., pp. 469–71.

24. Ibid., pp. 469–71. It is interesting to note that this asymmetry in the treatment of the postulates *reverses* one that predominated in the *Critique*, where transcendent freedom was said to be only tenuously required for morality, but God and immortality strictly so (A803–13 / B831–41; Kant already changed his mind by the time of writing the preface of the second edition, however—see Bxxvii–Bxxx).

25. It is not clear that Kant *consistently* adheres to this new position in the writings of the 1790s. The *Prize Essay* of 1791 seems closer to the position of the *Critique*. The *Metaphysics of Morals* (1797) does characterize morality as *Wissen* and does envisage a *Wissenschaft* concerned with morality (AA 6:375, 410–13), but does not contain an account of the postulates.

26. Cf. *Critique*, A551 / B579, including note a.

CHAPTER ELEVEN
FAILURES OF SELF-REFLECTION

1. This is clear, first, from the *necessity* which they involve (or, equivalently, their assertion that such and such is a condition of the *possibility* of experience). For Kant famously holds that a proposition's necessity is a sufficient condition of its a priority (*Critique*, B3: "If we have a proposition which in being thought is thought as *necessary*, it is an *a priori* judgment"). Second, it is also clear from the fact that Kant evidently regards all of the (essential) contents of the *Critique* as a priori (ibid., Axv).

2. For example, A. C. Ewing, J. Bennett, and R.C.S. Walker have taken these propositions to be *analytic*, whereas L. W. Beck takes them to be *synthetic*.

3. See, for example, *Prolegomena*, pp. 294–7, 308, 312–13, 316–17, 320.

4. This point must not be confused with the quite different—and entirely fallacious—thought that if some proposition q is analytically

implied by another proposition p, then q must itself be analytic. Counterexample: Smith is a bachelor, therefore Smith is unmarried.

5. See *Critique*, A202 / B247, B289, A259 / B315; *Prolegomena*, pp. 312–13.

6. See, for example, *Prolegomena*, 276–8: "Metaphysics stands or falls with the solution to this problem [How are synthetic propositions a priori possible?]; its very existence depends upon it. Let anyone make metaphysical assertions with ever so much plausibility, let him overwhelm us with conclusions; but if he has not first been able to answer this question satisfactorily, I have the right to say: this is all vain, baseless philosophy and false wisdom . . . All metaphysicians are . . . solemnly and legally suspended from their occupations until they shall have satisfactorily answered the question: How are synthetic cognitions a priori possible? For the answer contains the only credentials which they must show when they have anything to offer us in the name of pure reason. But if they do not possess these credentials, they can expect nothing else of reasonable people, who have been deceived so often, than to be dismissed without further ado." Also, *Critique*, A3–4 / B7–8, A209–10 / B255, A233 / B285–6.

7. Any move to stop this infinite regress by resorting to circularity at some point would obviously involve *vicious* circularity.

8. To my best knowledge, I invented this criticism (some ten or fifteen years ago). It has been circulating in drafts of this essay for many years and was in particular present in the draft submitted to the press in 2005. I was recently shocked and saddened to discover an article published by another author in 2006 which contains what seems to be an abbreviated and garbled version of it, presented without the proper attribution. (The article also shows several further signs of familiarity with this essay, again unacknowledged.)

9. For example, at *Prolegomena*, p. 276, n. 6 he says that in giving these explanations "we often use nothing but synthetic propositions, as in mathematical analysis," and his very inclusion of them in metaphysics and in the *Critique* marks them as a priori.

10. Consider again Kant's strictures at *Prolegomena*, pp. 276–8 (as recently quoted in note 6); and also *Critique*, A3–4 / B7–8, A209–10 / B255, A233 / B285–6.

11. For this central doctrine, see, e.g., *Critique*, Bxx, xxv–xxvi, A42–3 / B59–60, A252–60 / B310–15. The latter of the two grounds for the doctrine mentioned here (Kant's theory of schematism) is especially conspicuous in the Phenomena and Noumena chapter and at A286–9 / B342–6.

12. For complaints similar to these ones, cf. Beck, "Toward a Meta-Critique of Pure Reason," in his *Essays on Kant and Hume*, and Walsh, *Reason and Experience*, ch. 9.

13. *Critique*, Axiv. Kant's suggestion here of a Cartesian self-transparency of the mind is indefensible within the framework of the critical philosophy, at least if understood as a doctrine about the mind and its activities *in themselves*, as it would have to be in order to explain our knowledge of the thesis of transcendental idealism.

14. Ibid., Bxvi–xxii.

15. Ibid., Bxviii, note a.

16. Ibid., Bxvi–xvii.

17. Ibid., Axv; cf. A769–82 / B797–810.

18. Ibid., Bxviii, note a; cf. A769–82 / B797–810.

19. Ibid., Bxxii, note a. Cf. *Prize Essay*, p. 268.

20. Kant seems to imply here that our success in referring by means of the a priori concepts of his new "metaphysics of nature" is more certain than our knowledge of its synthetic a priori principles.

21. *Critique*, Bxviii, including note a; Bxx; A506–7 / B534–5.

22. The Antinomies would still be available as arguments in its support. However, it seems unlikely that they could plausibly bear the burden of proof by themselves. Indeed, Kant's tendency to cast them in a merely supporting role in this connection amounts to acknowledging as much.

23. *Critique*, A69–70 / B94–5. Kant says the following at *Mrongovius Metaphysics*, p. 803 concerning the analogous case of the a priori concepts of the understanding: "In every system a gap reveals itself if even the slightest thing is missing, because an idea of the whole is the basis there. When we have a sand heap we do not see if a few grains are missing, but when we have a pyramid, then straightaway. Just this occurs when we sketch a system of the categories as well." Cf. R. Brandt, *Die Urteilstafel* (Hamburg: Felix Meiner, 1991), p. 59.

24. Cf. *Critique*, A304 / B360–1.

25. See Brandt, *Die Urteilstafel*. Brandt also notes that there seems to be an intended correlation of I, II, and III with, respectively, the subject in a subject-predicate judgment, the copula, and the predicate. However, this idea seems much less promising. For example, how could it warrant the inclusion of hypothetical and disjunctive judgments under III?

26. *Critique*, A68–9 / B93–4.

27. The suggestion that this is all that Kant has to say in answer to the problem of horizontal exhaustiveness would be vigorously disputed by some interpreters, in particular by Klaus Reich and his followers.

In his influential book *The Completeness of Kant's Table of Judgments*
(Stanford: Stanford University Press, 1992; originally published in
German in 1932) Reich argues that Kant in the *Critique* implicitly has
a far more elaborate strategy for establishing the horizontal exhaustiveness of his four groups of forms of judgment, namely one of showing that the existence of all and only these groups is implied by the
very "definition" of a "judgment" (pp. 47, 102). However, as far as I
can see, Kant actually has no such strategy, at least not in the *Critique*.
This seems clear from the following facts (some further criticisms can
be found in work by L. Krüger, R. Brandt, and M. Wolff): (1) As Reich
himself concedes (p. 108), Kant nowhere explicitly advances such a
strategy in the *Critique*. (2) Reich explains its absence from the work
in terms of Kant's statement at *Critique*, A13–14 / B27–8 that, although
the work will completely enumerate all of the fundamental concepts
which contribute to a priori knowledge, it will not exhaustively analyze
them or review those which can be derived from them (pp. 108–9).
This explanation is unconvincing, however. For in the passage in question Kant is merely saying that the work will exclude certain analyses
which are *not crucial* for its position, not, as Reich's explanation would
require, analyses which *are* crucial for it. (3) Just before the section in
the *Critique* which presents the logical forms of judgment, Kant says
that the section will show that giving "an exhaustive statement of the
functions of unity in judgments . . . can quite easily be done" (A69 /
B94). So Kant clearly thinks that his demonstration of their exhaustion
is *easy* and *evident in this section of the text*, not a *difficult* and *hidden*
demonstration such as Reich hypothesizes. (4) Kant in the *Critique*
presents the fact that we have "just these and no other functions of
judgment" as a paradigmatic example of a fact not "capable of further
explanation" (B145–6). However, if Reich's conception of the analytic
derivability of all and only these functions of judgment from the very
concept of a "judgment" were Kant's, then the fact in question *would*
be further explicable. (5) Kant seems to preclude Reich's strategy as
one that would be positively unacceptable to him in the following
passage of the *Critique*: "No concept given a priori . . . can, strictly
speaking, be defined. For I can never be certain that the clear representation of a given concept, which as given may still be confused, has
been completely effected, unless I know that it is adequate to its object.
But since the concept of it may, as given, include many representations,
which we overlook in our analysis, although we are constantly
making use of them in our application of the concept, the completeness of the analysis of my concept is always in doubt . . . Instead of the
term definition, I prefer to use the term *exposition*, as being a more

guarded term, which the critic can accept as being up to a certain point valid, though still entertaining doubts as to the completeness of the analysis . . . Philosophical definitions are never more than expositions of given concepts . . . [which] can be obtained only by analysis (the completeness of which is never apodeictically certain)" (A728–30 / B756–8). One problem which this passage poses for Reich's interpretation concerns his use of the notion of a "definition" of judgment, for the passage shows that this would be unacceptable to Kant. Another, and more serious, problem is that the passage seems clearly to reject the idea, central to Reich's whole strategy, that the analysis of an a priori concept such as "judgment" can establish the *exhaustiveness* of the elements resulting from the analysis. In sum, Reich's strategy is not Kant's.

M. Wolff, *Die Vollständigkeit der kantischen Urteilstafel* (Frankfurt am Main: Vittorio Klostermann, 1995) develops a very sophisticated variant of Reich's approach. However, it seems vulnerable to similar objections. (1) Wolff rightly faults Reich for locating the argument which he attributes to Kant outside of the *Critique*. But Wolff's own attempt to excavate it from the short stretch of text at A67–70 / B92–5 involves such a massive interpolation of tacit premises and steps of inference as to be hardly less exegetically implausible (recall that Kant says at A69 / B94 that the relevant section of the *Critique* will show that giving a demonstration of the exhaustion of the functions of judgment "can quite easily be done"). (2) Wolff's interpretation relies on a very implausible reading of Kant's assertion at B145–6 that the fact that we have just these and no other forms of judgment is not "capable of further explanation." On Wolff's reading this in effect merely means not "capable of further explanation *than the ambitious one I have already given*" (*Die Vollständigkeit*, pp. 180–1). (3) In addition, some of the details of the argument that Wolff attributes to Kant are, to say the least, very surprising. For example, on Wolff's interpretation "I Quantity" turns out to be concerned with differences in *predicate*-concepts (ibid., pp. 143–4), whereas it is clearly for Kant rather concerned with differences in *subject*-concepts (see, e.g., Kant's *Logic*, p. 102).

28. Cf. Reich, *The Completeness of Kant's Table of Judgments*, pp. 103 ff., which already develops the germ of the following interpretation.

29. *Reflexion* no. 5854 from the 1780s states: "There are therefore three logical functions [elementary and not derivative] under a certain head, and hence three categories also: two of the functions manifest the unity of consciousness as regards two opposites, but the third function mutually connects the consciousness again. No more kinds of the

unity of consciousness can be thought. For there is (a) one consciousness which combines a manifold, (b) another consciousness which combines in an opposite way, and so (c) is the combination of (a) and (b)" (AA 18, no. 5854; cf. *Critique*, B110–11).

30. Thus in the *Critique* itself Kant writes in a similar spirit to *Reflexion* no. 5854 concerning the analogous case of the a priori concepts of the understanding, but adds this point about non-analyzability due to elementariness, or primitiveness: "It is significant that in each class the number of the categories is always the same, namely, three. Further, it may be observed that the third category in each class always arises from the combination of the second category with the first . . . It must not be supposed, however, that the third category is therefore merely a derivative, and not a primary, concept of the pure understanding. For the combination of the first and second concepts, in order that the third may be produced, requires a special act of the understanding, which is not identical with that which is exercised in the case of the first and the second" (B110–11).

31. Cf. *Critique*, A71 / B96, and B111 on the corresponding a priori concepts. (Since Kant correlates the universal form of judgment with *unity* and the *singular* with totality, he would himself express what I have here put in terms of *totality* rather in terms of *unity*. However, it seems very plausible to say that he gets the correlations the wrong way round. And in any case the difference does not affect my main point here much.)

32. Cf. ibid., B111 on the corresponding a priori concepts.

33. Concerning the non-analyzability here, cf. Walker, *Kant*, pp. 26–7.

34. Cf. *Critique*, A73–4 / B98–9.

35. In order to see the obstacles in the way of analysis here, it is important to realize that for Kant (1) disjunctive judgments are *aut* judgments rather than *vel* judgments, "p or q" here in effect meaning (p v q) & -(p & q), and (2) hypothetical judgments are not merely judgments of material implication (p ⊃ q as logically equivalent to -(p & -q)) but instead include a robust notion of consequence (*Konsequenz*).

36. See *Critique*, A74–5 / B100.

37. Ibid., B111: "Necessity is just the existence which is given through possibility itself." Cf. B4, where Kant defines strict universality as a matter of thinking something "in such a manner that no exception is allowed as possible," and says that in this sense of strict universality it and necessity "are inseparable from one another."

38. Note in particular that the reality expressed here is arguably not quite the same as that expressed by an assertoric judgment, in that here it can be ascribed to merely possible cases (e.g., the necessity that the internal angles of a triangle sum to 180 degrees consists in the fact that all possible triangles—whether they are actual or *merely possible*—*really* have internal angles that sum to 180 degrees).

39. Notice, incidentally, that this interpretation of Kant's strategy for establishing vertical exhaustiveness enables one to see it as the original inspiration of the dialectical method subsequently developed by Fichte and Hegel, who likewise employed it in the service of demonstrating entire systematicity and thence complete collection. In their dialectical method Fichte and Hegel reiterated Kant's basic model of two opposites leading to a non-analyzable synthesis at successive levels, and then used circularity in the resulting chain as the criterion that an entire system had been achieved.

40. *Critique*, A74 / B99–100; cf. A219 / B266, A233–5 / B286–7.

41. Of course, an alternative rationale for including the modal forms of judgment might be found—for example, their fundamental role in the distinctive forms of inference treated by modal logic.

42. *Critique*, A126, A132 / B171.

43. Ibid., A106, A141–2 / B180–1.

44. Ibid., A132 / B171.

45. Ibid., A132–3 / B171–2.

46. The reduction would be: p vel q = (-p ⊃ q) & (-q ⊃ p). Such a reduction would only "arguably" be possible, because it would require accepting Kant's apparent assumption that conjunction can somehow be taken for granted.

47. Cf. Brandt, *Die Urteilstafel*, p. 88. Brandt notes that Lambert had already included copulative judgments among the fundamental bases of inference (p. 102, n. 5).

48. *Critique*, Bviii.

49. M. Wolff in his very thought-provoking book *Die Vollständigkeit der kantischen Urteilstafel* attempts to forestall this sort of objection by arguing (a) that for Kant general logic is restricted to propositions which only employ general terms, (b) that Kant himself distinguishes between such a general logic and special logics, such as that devoted to forms of inference peculiar to mathematics, and that Frege's logic counts as an example of the latter rather than the former, and (c) that if Kant's general logic omits certain forms of inference which Frege's logic recognizes, the converse is also true. However, I think that one should be skeptical of this defense. Ad (a), even if Fregean quantificational logic is not *restricted* to propositions which employ only general

terms (because it admits proper names), it still recognizes many forms of inference which do only employ general terms but which are not accounted for by Kant. Ad (b), while it is certainly true that Frege's logic is especially adapted and suited to the needs of mathematics, it also captures many forms of inference involving multiple occurrences of quantification within a proposition which are implicitly used and recognized as valid in *everyday discourse* but which Kant's general logic omits. Ad (c), the arguable fact that Kantian logic's omission of forms of inference which are included by Fregean logic is complemented by a converse omission does nothing to diminish the former omission, which seems sufficient by itself to show that Kant's table of forms of judgment is incomplete.

CHAPTER TWELVE
THE PYRRHONIST'S REVENGE

1. The representative of the Kantian reading of Pyrrhonism with whom Hegel directly took issue was the neo-Kantian self-proclaimed "skeptic" G. E. Schulze rather than Kant himself.

2. My qualification "virtually" flags the fact that Hegel makes one exception: in its highest form, ancient Pyrrhonism did not, according to him, attack the position of true philosophy. This exception need not concern us here, however.

3. See M. F. Burnyeat, "Can the Skeptic Live His Skepticism?" in *The Skeptical Tradition*. For an adjudication of this interpretive dispute in which I basically favor the Hegel-Burnyeat reading of Pyrrhonism over the Kant-Frede reading, see my "Hegelian vs. Kantian Interpretations of Pyrrhonism: Revolution or Reaction?" in *Kritisches Jahrbuch der Philosophie*, vol. 10 (2005).

4. *Blomberg Logic*, pp. 210, 213–16.

5. Ibid., p. 216.

6. Diogenes Laertius, *Lives of Eminent Philosophers* (Cambridge, Mass.: Harvard University Press, 1979), vol. 2, ch. 9, sec. 102: "The dogmatists answer [the Pyrrhonian skeptics] by declaring that the skeptics themselves do apprehend and dogmatize; for when they are thought to be refuting their hardest they do apprehend, for at the very same time they are asseverating and dogmatizing. Thus even when they declare that they determine nothing, and that to every argument there is an opposite argument, they are actually determining these very points and dogmatizing."

7. Sextus Empiricus, *Outlines of Pyrrhonism*, bk. 1, chs. 1, 7, 11, 33. Of course, one might still raise questions about the tenability of this stance—as, for example, Burnyeat does in "Can the Skeptic Live His Skepticism?" But they will not be *Kant's* questions, and so I shall not pursue them here.

8. I say "a fortiori" here both because judgments of objective experience have traditionally seemed, and perhaps really are, easier to attack than judgments of subjective experience—this was Hegel's own reason for thinking in "a fortiori" terms—and because the former seem to presuppose the latter.

9. "No skeptic denies that there are in man intuitions, concepts, or ideas, or that these are distinct from one another. This is a matter of fact" (G. E. Schulze, *Aenesidemus, oder über die Fundamente der von dem Herrn Prof. Reinhold in Jena gelieferten Elementarphilosophie, nebst einer Verteidigung gegen die Anmaßungen der Vernunftkritik* [published anonymously and without specification of place of publication, 1792], pp. 100–1; cf. p. 45).

10. Thus Hegel writes that Pyrrhonism "through its turning against knowledge in general . . . finds itself, because it here opposes one thinking to another and combats the 'is' of philosophical thinking, driven likewise to overcome the 'is' of its own thinking" (G.W.F. Hegel, *Jenaer Schriften* [Frankfurt am Main: Suhrkamp, 1977], p. 248; cf. p. 254).

11. See, for instance, the Pyrrhonian "tropes of Aenesidemus" (as preserved in Sextus Empiricus, *Outlines of Pyrrhonism* and elsewhere).

12. Sextus Empiricus, *Against the Logicians* (Cambridge, Mass.: Harvard University Press, 1983), bk. 1, sec. 369.

13. Cf. Sextus's attack on the existence of sense-impressions which follows immediately afterwards in *Against the Logicians*. This additional material both provides further examples of counterarguments against judgments of subjective experience and also addresses a possible objection to my interpretation here, namely that Sextus's invocation of Democritus was intended in a less radical spirit than I imply, not as an attack on judgments of subjective experience but merely as an attack on judgments about the sensibly apparent objective world.

14. See, for example, *Outlines of Pyrrhonism*, bk. 1, ch. 10.

15. For example, Galen reports on the existence of a group of extreme Pyrrhonists who questioned even their own affections and whether or not we think (C. G. Kühn, *Galeni Opera Omnia* [Leipzig: C. Knobloch, 1821–33], 8:711, cf. 14:628; K. Deichgräber, *Die Griechische Empirikerschule* [Berlin: Weidmann, 1930], p. 133).

The evidence which I have just cited from Sextus and Galen seems to me to constitute a much better basis for a claim that the ancient Pyrrhonists levelled an equipollence attack even against subjective experience than the evidence to which Hegel himself tends to point in *The Relation of Skepticism to Philosophy*, namely the tropes of Aenesidemus.

16. According to Sextus, the skeptic does not refrain from all avowal, "for the skeptic assents to the feelings necessitated in sense-impression, and he would not, for example, say when feeling hot or cold 'I think that I do not feel hot or cold' "; the appearance or sense-impression, "since [it] lies in feeling and involuntary affection . . . is not open to question" (*Outlines of Pyrrhonism*, bk. 1, chs. 7, 11; Bury's translation slightly amended).

Similarly, the core of Descartes's case against skepticism in the *Meditations* and elsewhere lies in an argument to the effect that one's current subjective experience necessitates belief in and knowledge of it—that it is necessarily the case that if one is in some mental state S having a character C then one believes and knows this (Bernard Williams has aptly called this Descartes's principle of *evidence*)—so that one's current subjective experience is immune to skeptical doubt.

17. Descartes has a closely related but distinct principle which might also be supposed to pose problems for skepticism about one's own current subjective experience: the principle that it is necessarily the case that if one believes oneself to be in a mental state S having a character C then one is in such a state and one's belief constitutes knowledge. (Bernard Williams has aptly called this Descartes's principle of *incorrigibility*; together with the principle of *evidence*, it constitutes what is sometimes known as Descartes's conception of the mind's self-transparency.) Someone might hope to counter a skeptic inclined to skepticism about his own current subjective experience by appealing to this principle, encouraging him to infer: "Since I at least *believe* that I am currently having subjective experiences X, Y, and Z, and since in addition the principle of incorrigibility is true, I must really currently *be* having subjective experiences X, Y, and Z." However, this sort of response to the skeptic again fails to be compelling in the end, and for reasons similar to the first two reasons which just thwarted the argument from the principle of evidence: First, the principle of incorrigibility assumed here is again just the sort of dogmatic principle that the Pyrrhonian skeptic is adept at undermining through counterargument. One attractive step in this direction would be to point to the phenomenon of self-deception, for example. Second, the other essential premise, "I believe that I am currently having subjective experiences X, Y, and Z," is again flagrantly question-begging in relation to such a

skeptic. For *belief* is itself a subjective experience, and so precisely the sort of thing whose current existence in himself he is proposing to call into question.

18. *Critique*, B131. Cf. Kant's assertion, quoted earlier, that when one is concerned with "reason itself and its pure thinking . . . to obtain complete cognition of these, there is no need to go far afield, since I come upon them in my own self" (ibid., Axiv).

19. Cf. ibid., B132.

20. AA 7:135: "The field of our sensible intuitions and sensations of which we are not conscious although we can without doubt infer that we have them, i.e., of *obscure* representations in man (and likewise in animals), is immeasurable, but on the other hand, those which are clear contain only infinitesimally few of their points which lie open to consciousness. On the great *map* of our mind only a few places are *illuminated*, so to speak."

21. Thus, enumerating a set of propositions which he considers valid beyond all doubt, Schulze writes in his *Aenesidemus* that "the touchstone of all that is true is general logic, and every reasoning about matters of fact can lay claim to correctness only to the extent that it conforms to the laws of logic" (p. 45).

22. Hegel accuses Bouterwek of being unfaithful to his own principle of only going as far in his philosophizing as the skeptic would allow "to the extent that he [Bouterwek] erects . . . on the basis that doubting is itself a thinking, the whole system of laws of thought, as logic. For, on the contrary, the consistent skeptic denies the concept of a [logical] law altogether" (*Jenaer Schriften*, p. 141).

23. Hegel's early interest in Bardili's work is shown by a letter from Schelling to Fichte of May 24, 1801, and also by Bardili's appearance in Hegel's 1801 essay *The Difference Between the Fichtean and Schellingian Systems of Philosophy*.

24. *Critique*, A54 / B78.

25. Ibid., Bviii.

26. In K. L. Reinhold, *Beiträge zur leichteren Übersicht des Zustandes der Philosophie beim Anfange des 19. Jahrhunderts* (Hamburg: F. Perthes, 1801–3).

27. Ibid., p. 83.

28. "The Kantian school has itself demanded an appropriate metaphysics for everything that is supposed to be scientific in each kind of human knowledge, in which the connection of this piece of knowledge with its a priori grounds should be developed. Is only logic alone to do without such a metaphysics, and yet be, and be called, a science, indeed quite pure science?" (ibid., p. 85).

29. Thus, Bardili points out that "Kant thought he had recognized that the dogmatists and skeptics had remained standing with their quarrels only on the territory of metaphysics; and that on the territory of logic on the contrary an eternal peace has always prevailed" (ibid., p. 88). And he asks rhetorically in response to this view of Kant's "whether it is really true that skepticism has only called into question the objective in human cognition, or has not on the contrary also more than once dared to attack the validity of the laws of our understanding themselves" (ibid., pp. 88–9).

30. C. G. Bardili sought to realize such a project in his *Grundriß der ersten Logik, gereinigt von den Irrtümern bisheriger Logiken überhaupt, der Kantischen insbesonders* [*Outline of the First Logic Purified of the Errors of Previous Logics in General and of the Kantian in Particular*] (Stuttgart: F.C. Löflund, 1800). Hegel sought to realize such a project in his *Science of Logic* with its—somewhat, and surely not coincidentally, similar—"total reconstruction" of logic (*Science of Logic* [New York: Humanities Press, 1976], p. 51), which, he says, has its "justification" in his *Phenomenology of Spirit* (ibid., p. 48).

31. *Outlines of Pyrrhonism*, bk. 2, secs. 134–203; *Against the Logicians*, bk. 2, secs. 300–481.

32. Cicero, *Academica* (Cambridge, Mass.: Harvard University Press, 1979), bk. 2, secs. 95–8. The word "lie" here should be understood in the broad sense "speak falsely" (a sense which Cicero's *mentior*, like the Greek *pseudomai* which stands behind it, can readily bear). A simpler version of the paradox that works at least as well is: "This statement is false."

It should be noted that on certain interpretations the laws of bivalence and excluded middle may be significantly different. However, I shall disregard the potential difference between them here.

33. Among the more serious proposals which the skeptic might exploit in this way, there have, for example, been various suggestions that the law of bivalence or excluded middle should be given up in order to solve perceived difficulties in mathematics (the intuitionists), in quantum mechanics, and in logic itself. For instance, in relation to logic, it has been proposed in response to Russell's Paradox (in a manner strikingly reminiscent of the Academic skeptic's argument) that Russell's paradoxical sentence which says that *the class of all non-self-membered classes is a member of itself* should be coped with by instituting a three-valued logic in which the law of bivalence or excluded middle disappears and assigning this Russellian sentence the middle truth-value. Again, Hilary Putnam has proposed in response to problems arising within quantum mechanics a logic which, while retaining the

law of excluded middle, gives up the distributive law: p & (q v r) ⊃ (p & q) v (p & r) (H. Putnam, "The Logic of Quantum Mechanics," in his *Mathematics, Matter and Method: Philosophical Papers, Volume 1* [Cambridge: Cambridge University Press, 1975]). Among the more hypothetical proposals which a skeptic might exploit are Wittgenstein's suggestion in the *Remarks on the Foundations of Mathematics* that one could respond to Russell's Paradox by dispensing with the law of contradiction in relation to the paradoxical Russellian sentence (L. Wittgenstein, *Remarks on the Foundations of Mathematics* [Oxford: Blackwell, 1978], pt. 4, par. 59), and Wittgenstein's slightly less dramatic suggestion in the *Philosophical Investigations* that one could adopt a logic in which double negations were treated either as meaningless or else as equivalent to single negations, so that, for example, the law of double-negation elimination disappeared (*Philosophical Investigations* [Oxford: Blackwell, 1976], par. 554).

34. It might be objected here that applying the equipollence method to logic in such a manner would require holding at least *one* logical law firm: the law of contradiction. For does not the equipollence method presuppose the necessity of avoiding contradictions? However, this objection is dubious. For one thing, it seems open to the skeptic to reject *particular* contradictions that come along without doing so on the basis of a commitment to a general *law* proscribing contradictions.

35. The question of the epistemological security of logical principles has in general received rather scandalously little attention from philosophers, who have tended, instead, to show indecent haste in attempting to reduce other sorts of principles to logical ones, on the assumption that the latter were certain and that their certainty would thereby transfer to the former as well—as, for example, in Kant's explanation of analyticity in terms of the law of contradiction, and Frege's attempt to reduce arithmetic to logic.

36. *Critique*, A52 / B76. Cf *Logic*, p. 13: logic is a "science of the necessary laws of thinking without which no use of the understanding and of reason takes place at all."

37. *Critique*, Bxxvi. Cf. *Prize Essay*, p. 325.

38. *Critique*, A291 / B348, emphasis added (Kant's formulation in this sentence is of course paradoxical, but only in an easily remediable way).

It is therefore a mistake to say—as Walsh does at *Reason and Experience*, pp. 98–9, 218, and as several more recent commentators do too—that for Kant logic is purely prescriptive. It *is* prescriptive for him, but it is so *in virtue of conformity to it being an essential feature of thought*, so that failure to conform to it entails ceasing to think. It is true that he says in his published *Logic* that in logic the question is "not how we think, but how we ought to think" (p. 14). But the context of this remark shows clearly that what he means by it is that logic is not about how we *contingently happen to* think. Again, ascribing this position to him does naturally prompt the question how he can accommodate the sorts of deviations from logic which seem not only to occur in practice but also to be required, at least as possibilities, if the conception of the discipline as prescriptive is to make sense. However, this should be raised as a real (and interesting) question, not a rhetorical one.

39. As Béatrice Longuenesse has pointed out to me, there are two passages in the *Critique* which might be thought to imply a further epistemological defense or justification of classical logic: at A117 Kant writes that "the possibility of the logical form of all cognition is necessarily conditioned by relation to . . . apperception as a faculty" (cf. B131), and at B133–4 he gives an argument to the conclusion that "the synthetic unity of apperception is . . . that highest point to which we must ascribe all employment of the understanding, even the whole of logic." As far as I can see, though, his point at A117 is merely that general logic presupposes the transcendental unity of apperception in the sense that, like all representations, those involved in logic must be ascribable to the self, and the point of his argument at B133–4 is merely that the general concepts which logic employs need to be abstracted from syntheses of representations of a sort that interdepend with such self-ascribability. In other words, there is no *defense* or *justification* of classical logic intended here. If there *were*, it would presumably just be that the transcendental unity of apperception, as essentially involving *thought* (cf. B157), essentially involves conformity to classical logic (i.e., it would merely be a variant of the defense which I have already attributed to Kant). Certainly, Kant's idea cannot coherently be that we can justify classical logic by *deducing* it from the transcendental unity of apperception.

40. Pace some recent claims by H. Putnam and his followers that it was.

41. *Metaphysics*, 1005b–1007a.

42. I have of course chosen these examples in part because they are all cases of rather *disciplined* deviations from and rejections of the law. But these are the right sorts of cases to consider. It is easy enough to make cases of merely *random* deviations and rejections look like examples of non-belief and non-thought. But then, merely random utterances of *any* kind tend to look like that, whether they violate classical logical principles or not.

43. For such an objection, see J. Barnes, "The Law of Contradiction," *Philosophical Quarterly*, vol. 19, no. 77 (1969), pp. 308–9.

44. *Metaphysics*, 1005b26–32.

45. Barnes embraces this line of argument, and elaborates on it at some length. But he too begs the original question, namely in assuming that belief and disbelief are contraries, so that it is necessarily true that, as he puts it, (x) ((xD:(P)) ⊃ (-xB:(P))), i.e., if anyone disbelieves ("D") a proposition P then he does not believe ("B") proposition P ("The Law of Contradiction," p. 304).

46. *Metaphysics*, 1006a11–1007a35.

47. In other words, this would at best only constitute an argument for what Putnam has called the *minimal* principle of contradiction: not every statement is both true and false (H. Putnam, "There is at least one a priori truth," in his *Realism and Reason: Philosophical Papers, Volume 3* [Cambridge: Cambridge University Press, 1983]). Incidentally, Putnam's own argument for such a principle is quite different from the one in question here. Note, in particular, that he would not be sympathetic to the appeal to analyticity made in the reconstruction suggested here.

48. G. F. Meier, *Vernunftlehre* (Halle: Johann Justinus Gebauer, 1752): logic is "a science that treats the rules that one must observe in order to think rationally" (p. 5; cf. p. 7); concerning the avoidance of contradictions, "It is contrary to the nature of our understanding to think otherwise. Who can imagine as possible that God exists and also doesn't exist, that all men can err and some cannot err?" (p. 548); "When one at the same time affirms and denies one and the very same thing of one and the very same thing, one thinks nothing" (p. 567); "A simply impossible cognition [such as dry snow or wooden iron] is . . . no cognition at all, but it only seems to be a cognition" (pp. 131–2; cf. p. 484).

49. *Metaphysics*, 1005a15–1006a15.

50. Thus at *Critique*, A59–60 / B83–4 Kant says that general logic furnishes criteria for truth, in the sense of necessary conditions for truth. But his ground for saying this is not an Aristotelian (or Fregean) assumption that logical laws hold for all being as such. Rather, it is that "whatever contradicts [*widerspricht*] these rules is false [*falsch*]. For the understanding would thereby be made to contradict its own general rules of thought, and so to war against itself. These criteria, however, concern only the form of truth, that is, of thought in general" (in interpreting this passage, it should be noted that *widerspricht* literally means *speaks* against, and that in German *falsch* often means not false but wrong in a broader sense). In other words, because conformity to gen-

eral logic is essential for thinking, failure to conform to it undermines the very existence of the acts of thought whose correspondence to objects constitutes truth on Kant's standard correspondence theory of truth. Cf. A150 / B189–90.

51. This assumption—which can in the end be traced back to Aristotle's position in *Metaphysics*, bk. theta that actuality is prior to potentiality—is perhaps most explicit in Kant's precritical essay *The Only Possible Argument in Support of a Demonstration of God's Existence* (1763), where it motivates positing God as the actual ground of all possibilities. At *Critique*, A579–83 / B607–11 Kant rejects that theological conclusion, *but not the assumption*, which on the contrary now motivates an empirical analogue of that conclusion, namely a principle that all empirical possibilities are grounded in the single reality of experience—a principle in terms of which Kant now seeks to explain the earlier theological conclusion as a sort of derivative illusion. The assumption in question also lies behind Kant's central critical-period project of explaining *synthetic a priori* necessities in terms of the actual fact of mind-imposition (i.e., in terms of transcendental idealism). Indeed, it is visible in his critical-period explanations of *both* of the only other two types of propositional necessity which he recognizes besides logical necessity: synthetic a priori necessity consists in *the actual fact of mind-imposition*, while analytic necessity (insofar as distinguishable from logical necessity) consists in *the actual fact of the containment of a predicate-concept by a subject-concept* (cf. ibid., B17: it is a matter of "what we *actually* think in [the given concept]").

52. See *Critique*, A54 / B78; *Logic*, p. 14.

53. In order to solve this problem while still retaining a version of the explanation, Kant would have had to arrive at conclusions which would at the very least have greatly surprised him. He recognizes just three types of necessity that might be of relevance here: logical necessity, the necessity of synthetic a priori principles, and the necessity of analytic principles (which he sometimes explains in terms of logic but sometimes in terms of the containment of a predicate-concept by a subject-concept). Obviously, the solution to his problem here could not be that the residual necessity in question was *logical* necessity. But nor would he be at all inclined to classify it as *synthetic a priori* necessity (since, for one thing, that would deprive general logic of its validity for *all* thought, rather than just human(-like) thought, given that he always explains theoretical synthetic a priori necessity in terms of the imposition of the principles involved by *minds like ours*). And so the only remotely attractive tack for him to take would be to say that it is instead an *analytic* necessity, grounded in the containment of a predi-

cate-concept by a subject-concept—in other words, to say, roughly, that it is a necessity constituted by the fact that the subject-concept "thought" implicitly contains the predicate-concept "conforms to classical logical principles." But saying this would require conceding to analyticity (in the sense of the containment of a predicate-concept by a subject-concept) a sort of primacy over logic which would at the very least greatly surprise Kant (who commonly, rather, explains analyticity in terms of logic, specifically in terms of the logical law of contradiction—see, e.g., *Critique*, A151 / B190–1).

54. Wittgenstein, *Remarks on the Foundations of Mathematics*, pt. 1, par. 131.

55. Wittgenstein, *Philosophical Investigations*, pp. 226e–7e.

56. Wittgenstein, *Remarks on the Foundations of Mathematics*, pt. 4, par. 59.

57. In his *Encyclopedia* Hegel calls classical logic "the logic of mere Understanding" (par. 82).

Index

hypothetical form of judgment,
42–3, 50, 71, 73–4

ideality of space and time, 23, 42–3
ideas: regulative, 35; transcendent,
117n31
immanent physiology. *See* metaphysics of nature
intuition: sensible vs. pure, 23, 34,
42, 114n8

Kant, I.: *Anthropology*, 81; *Blomberg Logic*, 19, 95n8, 101n10, 102n18,
103nn19 and 21, 123nn13–14,
138nn4–5; *Critique of Judgment*,
20, 61, 104n27, 128n8, 131nn22–
4; *Critique of Practical Reason*, 20,
61, 95nn9 and 12, 104nn27 and 3,
130nn19–21; *Critique of Pure Reason*, passim; *Dohna Metaphysics*,
112n38, 120n12; *Dreams of a Spirit Seer, Illustrated by Dreams of Metaphysics*, ix, 18–19, 22–3, 38, 60, 63,
100n6, 101–2n12, 102nn13–17,
103nn20–1, 105–6nn5–6, 107nn8
and 10, 108n22, 111n35,
129nn12–13; *Groundwork of the Metaphysics of Morals*, 61,
129nn14–15, 130n18; *Herder Logic*, 103n19; *Herder Metaphysics*,
108nn21–2, 109n28; *Inaugural Dissertation*, 23–4, 95n7, 100n5,
108nn22 and 26, 109n28, 119n9,
120n10, 121n17, 122n4, 129n14;
Inquiry Concerning the Distinctness of the Principles of Natural Theology and Morality, 106n7, 117n29; letter
to Bernouilli (1781), 17–18; letter
to Garve (1798), 14–17, 23, 33,
117n33; letter to Herz (1772), 24–
5, 28, 30–2, 42, 107nn16–19,
120nn10 and 13; letter to Mendelssohn (1766), 22, 100n10; *Logic*, 59,
128nn9–11, 135n27, 143n36,
144n38, 146n52; *Metaphysical*

Foundations of Natural Science,
114n13, 123n20; *Metaphysics of Morals*, 129nn12 and 14, 131n25;
Mrongovius Metaphysics, 94–5n3,
109nn27 and 30, 115n20, 116n24,
118n3, 119n8, 130n17, 133n23;
New Elucidation, 6–7, 9–10, 99-
100n4; *Notice concerning the Structure of Lectures in the Winter Semester 1765–1766*, 18, 98n3, 100n10,
101n11, 105–6n5; *Observations on the Feeling of the Beautiful and the Sublime*, 100–1n10; *On A Discovery*, 11, 122n4; *The Only Possible Argument In Support of A Demonstration of God's Existence*, 99n4,
146n51; open letter on Fichte's
Wissenschaftslehre, 30, 125n26; *Philippi Logic*, 103n19; *Philosophical Encyclopedia*, 117n33; *Physical Monadology*, 99n4, 100n6, 106n7;
Pölitz Metaphysics, 128n6, 129n12;
Prize Essay on Progress in Metaphysics, 11, 14, 98n8, 103n23, 113n3,
114nn6 and 9, 115–16nn17, 21,
and 24, 117n28, 123n21, 125n26,
126nn27, 1 and 3, 127n5, 128n5,
131n25, 133n19, 143n37, *Prolegomena to Any Future Metaphysics*,
passim; *Reflexionen*, 95n7, 96n20,
101n10, 108n23 and 26, 135n29;
Religion Within the Limits of Reason Alone, 20, 104n27; *Universal Natural History and Theory of the Heavens*, 99n4, 108n22; *Volckmann Metaphysics*, 104n3, 120n11,
123n19, 126nn27 and 29; *Von Schön Metaphysics*, 50, 109n29,
114n14, 115n16, 116nn21–2,
117n28, 121n13, 124–5n24,
126n26
Kemp Smith, N., x, 107n20, 128n7
knowledge (*Wissen*), 46–9, 58–62,
128nn7–12, 129–31nn16–22
and 25